OECD Reviews on Local Job Creation

Indigenous Employment and Skills Strategies in Canada

This work is published under the responsibility of the Secretary-General of the OECD. The opinions expressed and arguments employed herein do not necessarily reflect the official views of OECD member countries.

This document, as well as any data and any map included herein, are without prejudice to the status of or sovereignty over any territory, to the delimitation of international frontiers and boundaries and to the name of any territory, city or area.

Please cite this publication as:
OECD (2018), *Indigenous Employment and Skills Strategies in Canada*, OECD Reviews on Local Job Creation, OECD Publishing, Paris.
http://dx.doi.org/10.1787/9789264300477-en

ISBN 978-92-64-30046-0 (print)
ISBN 978-92-64-30047-7 (PDF)

Series: OECD Reviews on Local Job Creation
ISSN 2311-2328 (print)
ISSN 2311-2336 (online)

The statistical data for Israel are supplied by and under the responsibility of the relevant Israeli authorities. The use of such data by the OECD is without prejudice to the status of the Golan Heights, East Jerusalem and Israeli settlements in the West Bank under the terms of international law.

Photo credits: Cover © Andy Dean Photography/Shutterstock.com;© BrianAJackson /iStock/Getty Images Plus

Corrigenda to OECD publications may be found on line at: *www.oecd.org/about/publishing/corrigenda.htm*.

Preface

Across many OECD countries, Indigenous People represent an important and growing demographic group with a unique set of cultures and customs. In a local development context, many Indigenous People are within remote areas and face unique challenges in finding quality employment and economic development opportunities. They often experience lower outcomes than the non-Indigenous population on a number of key economic and social indicators.

Well-designed employment and skills policies are fundamental to link Indigenous People to high quality jobs, while also contributing to broader economic development objectives and inclusive growth. The OECD LEED Programme has built a large body of evidence on "what works" for disadvantaged groups, including Indigenous populations over the past 35 years. This work has demonstrated the importance of providing more autonomy to the local level to enable policy innovation. With regard to Indigenous People, this is critical in supporting the principle of self-determination.

In consideration of the Truth and Reconciliation Commission of Canada's Calls to Action, this report is set within the context of furthering the restoration of Indigenous rights at the national, regional and local level. To do so, this report analyses employment, education, job creation and local development outcomes of Indigenous People within Canada. After determining the barriers preventing Indigenous People from reaching better outcomes, the report proposes potential ways forward for Indigenous labour market and skills programming.

With this report, the OECD hopes to place Indigenous voices at the forefront of the discussion and looks to Indigenous communities as the leaders of local, regional and national change.

I would like to warmly thank Employment and Social Development Canada for their active participation and support of the study, and for their ongoing partnership with the OECD. I would also like to sincerely thank the Indigenous organisations that actively participated in this study and provided critical feedback on the report.

Lamia Kamal-Chaoui

Director, Centre for Entrepreneurship, SMEs, Regions and Cities

Foreword

Ensuring that Indigenous People have access to quality job opportunities that align with their unique cultural identity is integral within on-going efforts to support inclusive growth in Canada. This report is part of overall work being conducted on Indigenous People within the OECD Centre for Entrepreneurship, SMEs, Regions, and Cities, considering how to best design local employment and skills strategies, as well as how to better link Indigenous communities to regional development efforts. This report builds on previous work conducted in Canada as part of the OECD Reviews on Local Job Creation of the LEED Programme, which looked at Indigenous employment and skills policies in the Yukon and Saskatchewan in 2016.

Over the past few years in Canada, the federal government's has repeatedly affirmed its commitment to renew its relationship with Indigenous People based on the recognition of rights, respect, co-operation and partnership. At the federal level, the majority of active labour market and skills programmes are managed by Employment and Social Development Canada (ESDC). ESDC has a suite of programmes which are delivered at the local level through the Indigenous Skills and Employment Training Strategy (ISETS) and Skills and Partnerships Fund (SPF). The federal government has conducted extensive engagement with Indigenous leaders, service delivery organisations, academic institutions and provincial and territorial governments to consider the best way forward to renew its active labour market programmes to ensure they are responsive to the needs of Indigenous People.

This report uses methodological triangulation to consider quantitative and qualitative data regarding employment, skills, and entrepreneurship opportunities for Indigenous People in Canada. It also takes a case study approach to better understand policies and programmes, which have demonstrated success in matching Indigenous People to jobs, while also building their skills and attracting new economic development opportunities.

Results from this study were discussed at the Community Economic Development (CED) annual event in September 2017, ECONOUS 2017, bringing together 380 delegates and community leaders across Canada. During this event, the OECD organised a workshop, which brought together Indigenous leaders, service delivery organisations, as well as federal and provincial government officials to discuss the key challenges facing Indigenous People and innovative programmes, which are achieving better outcomes.

In-depth interviews and analysis were undertaken across four case studies, which are implementing organisations of the ISETS: 1) Centre for Aboriginal Human Resources and Development (CAHRD): 2) Community Futures Treaty Seven; 3) MAWIW Council; and 4) Kiikenomaga Kikenjigewen Employment and Training Services (KKETS). In Canada, the realities of Indigenous People have to be examined along four distinct groupings including First Nations on-reserve, First Nations off-reserve, Inuit, and Metis. These case studies are primarily focused on First Nations off-reserve to provide valuable insights that can inform policy making on Indigenous programmes within urban areas in Canada. The results show the importance of fostering Indigenous leadership and providing Indigenous People with high quality job opportunities. It should be acknowledged that there are some limitations to the lessons that can be drawn given the unique diversity of Indigenous communities across Canada.

Acknowledgements

This report has been prepared by the Centre for Entrepreneurship, SMEs, Regions and Cities (CFE), led by Lamia Kamal-Chaoui, Director. This work was conducted as part of the OECD's Local Economic and Employment Development (LEED) Programme.

The project on local employment and skills strategies for Indigenous communities was coordinated by Jonathan Barr, Head of the Employment and Skills Unit within the Local Employment, Skills and Social Innovation (LESI) Division of CFE under the supervision of Sylvain Giguère, Head of Division.

The principal authors are Jonathan Barr and Lindsey Ricker (OECD). Charles Cirtwill and Dharmjot (DJ) Grewal from the Northern Policy Institute drafted sections of the report pertaining to Kiikenomaga Kikenjigewen Employment & Training Services and MAWIW Council. Beatriz Jambrina Canseco (OECD) provided valuable statistical and data analysis support.

Several OECD colleagues provided important feedback and advice on the development of this report, including Chris McDonald, CFE; Lorena Figueiredo, CFE; Rowan Phair, Directorate for Education and Skills (EDU); Andrew Barker, Economics Department (ECO); Glenda Quintini, Directorate for Employment, Labour and Social Affairs (ELS); and Katharine Mullock, ELS. Special thanks are also extended to Théa Chubinidze for formatting the report, Cicely Dupont-Nivore for preparing the report for publication and to Pauline Arbel for preparing the cover page.

Special thanks should be given to local stakeholders and Indigenous groups in each of the case study areas that participated in meetings and provided documentation and comments critical to the production of the report. In particular, the OECD is grateful to Community Futures Treaty Seven, the Centre for Aboriginal Human Resources Development Inc. (CAHRD), MAWIW Council and Kiikenomaga Kikenjigewen Employment and Training Services (KKETS) for their insights and contributions to this project. Additional thanks should be given to Ali Jalayer from the Department of Jobs and Small Business, Australia who participated in the OECD study visit to foster knowledge sharing between countries.

The OECD is also grateful to those individuals who participated in a workshop on Empowering Indigenous Communities through Stronger Local Economic and Employment Development in Calgary, Alberta as part of ECONOUS 2017, the annual event organised by Community Economic Development Network.

Lastly, appreciation should also be given to federal officials in Canada who contributed to this report and participated in the OECD study visits: Saloie Moreno, Claude Bazinet, Jean François LaRue; Stefan Bergeron, Tony Haddad, Robert Langlois, of Employment and Social Development Canada.

Table of contents

Figures

Boxes

Follow OECD Publications on:
http://twitter.com/OECD_Pubs
http://www.facebook.com/OECDPublications
http://www.linkedin.com/groups/OECD-Publications-4645871
http://www.youtube.com/oecdilibrary
http://www.oecd.org/oecddirect/
This book has...
StatLinks
A service that delivers Excel® files from the printed page!
Look for the StatLinks at the bottom of the tables or graphs in this book. To download the matching Excel® spreadsheet, just type the link into your Internet browser, starting with the http://dx.doi.org prefix, or click on the link from the e-book edition.

Reader's Guide

Building on the policy experience analysed over the past decades, the OECD has worked with member countries to elaborate a project to identify comparative best practices and programme principles, which can help **guide employment and skills policies, as well as the design of local strategies targeted to Indigenous People,** and integrate them with stronger **economic development and entrepreneurship initiatives**.

Each country report reviews policy actions in the following key areas:

- **Developing the skills of Indigenous People to better link them to jobs:** In many OECD countries, the overall educational attainment of Indigenous People falls significantly behind the non-Indigenous population. Skills are a key route out of poverty and provide a solid foundation for Indigenous People to participate in the labour market. The project considers how best to design skills development programmes, which better link Indigenous People to jobs;
- **Boosting the job creation potential of Indigenous People:** Attracting inward investments into Indigenous communities require a clear investment environment as well as incentives for businesses to locate in a region. This requires many communities to encourage entrepreneurship and provide business development support services. The project considers how to better encourage endogenous growth within Indigenous communities through stronger entrepreneurship opportunities as well as Indigenous SMEs development programmes;
- **Better designing programmes, which mutually reinforce Indigenous employment and economic development:** High levels of unemployment among Indigenous People can be addressed through better active labour market programmes which are customised to local labour market needs. The project considers the optimal role of employment services in matching Indigenous People to quality jobs, and
- **Getting local governance right:** The success of any programme or policy depends on having optimal governance frameworks and coordination at the national and local level, which provides incentives for policy innovation. The project considers how best to design national policies in a manner which rewards local innovation in Indigenous employment and economic development.

Project approach for Canada

This study and report presents a range of employment, skills, entrepreneurship and economic development indicators to show the economic and social outcomes of Indigenous People in Canada. The report also focuses on key programmes and policies. In-depth interviews and analysis were undertaken across four case study areas:

- **Centre for Aboriginal Human Resource Development (CAHRD),** based in Winnipeg, Manitoba, provides employment, adult and post-secondary education, trades training, day care facilities, and student transitional housing services to prepare

Indigenous People to be self-reliant and adaptable to the labour market and employment, serving all Indigenous People in Winnipeg, Manitoba;

- **Community Futures Treaty 7 (CFT7),** based in the province of Alberta, supports all First Nation individuals to obtain and maintain meaningful employment based on community needs through the provision of training in the Treaty Seven catchment area;
- **MAWIW Council** in Elsipogtog First Nation, New Brunswick supports and promotes the empowerment of First Nation's People residing within the organisation's service area, providing the appropriate training to HR staff to ensure proper delivery of services to achieve self-sufficiency and independence through counseling, training, and employment, providing resources to its communities, and
- **Kiikenomaga Kikenjigewen Employment and Training Services (KKETS),** in Thunder Bay, Ontario, assists Indigenous People prepare for, acquire and maintain successful employment by providing demand-driven education, training and employment opportunities through partnerships with community, education institutions, business/industry and government.

It is important to note that three of these case studies focus mostly on First Nations communities. In Canada, the realities of Indigenous Peoples have to be examined along four distinct groupings for analytical purposes. These include: First Nations on-reserve, First Nations off-reserve, Inuit, and Metis. They are four very distinct realities. As such, these case studies do provide valuable best practices and useful insights that can inform policy making, recognizing however, they may not reflect the results for all Indigenous communities in Canada.

Acronyms and Abbreviations

APS	Aboriginal Peoples Survey
ASETS	Aboriginal Skills Employment and Training Strategy
BDC	Business Development Bank of Canada
BEST	(Aboriginal) Business and Entrepreneurship Skills Training
CAUAC	Calgary Aboriginal Urban Affairs Committee
CBP	Canadian Business Patterns
CCAE	Canadian Centre for Aboriginal Entrepreneurship
CCB	Canada Child Benefit
CFP	Community Futures Program
CIDI	Canadian Institute of Diversity and Inclusion
CMA	Census Metropolitan Area
CRA	Canadian Revenue Agency
ECEC	Early Childhood Education and Care
ERG	Employee Resource Groups
ESDC	Employment and Social Development Canada
FNSI	First Nations Statistical Institute
FMM	First Ministers Meeting
ICT	Information, Communications and Technology
INAC	Indigenous and Northern Affairs Canada
ISIA	Intergovernmental Strategic Indigenous Alignment
LED	Lands and Economic Development
LEED	Local Economic and Employment Development
LFS	Labour Force Survey
LMI	Labour Market Information
MDSA	Municipal Development Service Agreements
MIAC	Mayor's Indigenous Advisory Circle
NEET	Not in Employment, Education or Training

NACCA	National Aboriginal Capital Corporations Association
NAICS	North American Classification Status
NGO	Non-Governmental Organisation
NHS	National Household Survey
OECD	Organisation for Economic Co-operation and Development
PIAAC	Programme for the International Assessment of Adult Competencies
PISA	Programme for International Student Assessment
POPCTR	Population Centre
PUMF	Public Use Microdata Files
RDA	Regional Development Agency
SES	Socio-Economic Status
SIN	Social Insurance Number
SME	Small and Medium-sized Enterprise
SPF	Skills and Partnerships Fund
SPI	Strategic Partnership Initiative
TRC	Truth and Reconciliation Commission of Canada
UNDRIP	United Nations Declaration on the Rights of Indigenous Peoples
VET	Vocational Education and Training

Executive Summary

Canada's Indigenous population, consisting of First Nations, Inuit and Métis, is a growing demographic group. In 2016, there were 1 673 785 Indigenous People in Canada, accounting for 4.9% of the total population. This was a substantial increase from 3.8% in 2006. According to Statistics Canada, since 2006, the Indigenous population has grown by 42.5% — more than four times the growth rate of the non-Indigenous population.

In addition to the overall growth, there has also been a significant movement of Indigenous People to urban places in Canada. From 2006 to 2016, the Indigenous population living in metropolitan areas of Canada increased by 59.7%. While population growth is occurring both on-reserve and off-reserve, 51.8% of the overall Indigenous population live in an urban setting.

Indigenous and non-Indigenous Canadians do not share the same labour market outcomes. In 2016, the unemployment rate for Indigenous people was 15.3%, compared to 7.4% for non-Indigenous People. Within Indigenous groups, unemployment was high for Inuit (22.4%) and First Nations (18%) relative to Métis (11.2%). Indigenous People also have lower levels of education and skills outcomes. In 2016, 40% of the Indigenous population completed postsecondary education, compared to 55.9% of the non-Indigenous population. Higher levels of skills are critical for Indigenous People as they lead to better quality and more productive jobs.

This report takes a case study approach to understand the implementation of Indigenous labour market and skills training programmes. A key success factor identified is that programmes are most successful when they delivered and managed by Indigenous People for Indigenous People. Several other factors have also been identified for continued success, including:

- **Governance through partnerships and engagement**: Effective governance is critical in making decisions that are informed, open, and transparent. Continuous engagement with Indigenous organisations to discuss workforce gaps and opportunities can ensure that all levels of government (federal, provincial, and municipal) ensure on-going improvements in the effectiveness of programmes and services to meet Indigenous Peoples' needs;
- **Access to culturally-sensitive services for urban Indigenous People:** Many non-Indigenous urban service delivery organisations do not necessarily provide culturally sensitive services to Indigenous People. Furthermore, information on where and how to access programmes and services is sometimes not readily available to urban Indigenous People. This situation can be especially challenging for Indigenous People who are moving from their community into an urban area. Programmes have the greatest chance of success when delivered in a culturally-sensitive manner;
- **Local leadership**: City mayors regularly participate in meetings with Indigenous communities; therefore, they have an important role to play in fostering trust. The examples from Winnipeg, Thunder Bay, Fredericton and Calgary show a clear leadership role being taken by the municipal government. These cities have strategic policy frameworks targeted to the urban Indigenous population, providing good examples that can be used for continuous improvement in other Canadian cities, and

- **Social capital and community-driven initiatives**: Social capital enhances local cooperation. The most significant improvements in the lives of Indigenous People come from within the community itself. Any policy or programme that seeks to improve the well-being of Indigenous People needs to ascertain how Indigenous People wish to define success in a local development context, based on the principles of reconciliation and self-determination.

Overall, the federal government is making strong efforts to reset the policy discourse around Indigenous People in Canada. Stronger partnerships with Indigenous communities based on open dialogue and learning can only favour better outcomes over the long term. This report makes the following recommendations:

- **Consider injecting additional flexibility into the management of Indigenous labour market and skills training programming:** This could be achieved by easing the reporting and accountability requirements on Indigenous service providers. It could also be achieved by establishing longer-term funding arrangements. The federal government's 2018 Budget announced the creation of the Indigenous Skills and Employment Training (ISET) Program, including 10 year funding agreements. This is a welcome development;
- **Continue work to improve alignment of federal and provincial Indigenous labour market programming:** It is critical to continue to build on the activities and successes in improving federal-provincial/territorial and Indigenous partnerships in the delivery of Indigenous programming, especially at the urban level in order to maximize effectiveness of efforts and investments;
- **Leverage the role of cities in addressing the needs of urban Indigenous People:** Cities can be policy spaces of opportunity to test new ideas and pilot new ways of partnering with Indigenous organisations. Urban Indigenous policies can have a stronger impact when designed in partnership with cities to ensure that urban zones are safe, rewarding, and productive environments for Indigenous People;
- **Improve the collection and use of Indigenous Labour Market Information (LMI):** Indigenous LMI could be enhanced through collaborations with Indigenous groups. The federal government should consider increasing investments in Indigenous specific LMI;
- **Look for opportunities to enhance skills training for Indigenous People through targeted work experience programmes:** ISET includes a greater focus on getting Indigenous People into higher quality jobs. To achieve this, it will be important to encourage and provide supports for life-long learning opportunities, especially for Indigenous Peoples who are already working;
- **Expand access to higher education opportunities to support Indigenous students:** The federal government should explore how to support the increase of successful completion of higher education by Indigenous Peoples, with the goal of increasing Indigenous employment within knowledge-based occupations;
- **Consider increasing the use of mentorship as a key tool for supporting Indigenous employment:** Increasing opportunities for Indigenous mentorship will lead to greater employee retention and build cultural awareness about Indigenous People in the workplace, and
- **Explore the use of social enterprises as a pathway to economic prosperity for Indigenous People:** Many Indigenous entrepreneurs cite substantial difficulties obtaining ample start-up funding. The federal government should continue to support and encourage the development of social enterprises as they often balance both social and profitability goals.

Chapter 1. Indigenous labour market outcomes in Canada

Disparities in labour force outcomes between Indigenous and non-Indigenous People can be addressed through more active labour market programmes, which involve a range of economic development actors. This chapter overviews key employment trends within the Indigenous population in Canada. It then outlines innovations of Indigenous organisations that are actively managing and delivering employment programmes, which seek to provide meaningful job opportunities to their Indigenous communities.

Recent population and labour market trends

The Truth and Reconciliation Commission of Canada (TRC) was established in 2008 in response to the systemic harm that the Residential School system inflicted on Indigenous People. In 2015, the TRC released its final report. In order to redress the legacy of Residential schools and advance the process of Canadian reconciliation, the report included 94 Calls to Action. These Calls to Action urged all levels of government, federal, provincial, territorial and Indigenous, to work together to change policies and programmes in order to repair the harm caused by Residential Schools and advance forward with reconciliation. (Truth and Reconciliation Commission of Canada, 2015).

One of the Calls to Action states that, "we call upon the federal government to develop with Aboriginal groups a joint strategy to eliminate educational and employment gaps between Aboriginal and non-Aboriginal Canadians" (Truth and Reconciliation Commission of Canada, 2015). The TRC observed that disparities in education and skills were closely tied with employment outcomes. While the government has made strides in prioritizing the rights and lives of Indigenous People, inequalities still remain and require multi-faceted policies to improve success (Truth and Reconciliation Commission of Canada, 2015).

The 2016 Census of Population and the 2011 National Household Survey (NHS) in Canada provide the most current and accurate portraits of the demographic and socio-economic conditions of Indigenous People in Canada. This report looks to the NHS, the Census, and other sources to ascertain how Indigenous People in Canada are currently fairing in the labour market. Indigenous outcomes are improving along several economic, social, and labour market indicators (Statistics Canada, 2017e).

Demographics and population trends

In 2011, First Nation People, Métis, and Inuit Indigenous groups comprised 4.3% of Canada's population (Statistics Canada, 2016a). Therefore, more than 1.4 million Canadians self-identified as Indigenous in the 2011 NHS (Statistics Canada, 2016a).

However, this number has grown considerably; between 2011 and 2016, Canada's total population grew by 4.9%, amounting to 34 460 065 people within the entire Canadian population as recorded by the 2016 Census. Simultaneously, the Indigenous population in Canada increased by 18%, with Statistics Canada documenting 1 673 780 Indigenous People within the 2016 Census (Statistics Canada, 2017a).

While the fertility rate of the entire Canadian population in 2011 was 1.6 children per woman (close to the OECD average of 1.7 children per woman), the Indigenous population in Canada had a fertility rate of 2.2 children per woman (Arriagada, 2016). In turn, the Indigenous population in Canada is growing at a far quicker pace than the rest of the Canadian population. This trend has been observed historically as well as there was a 20.1% increase in the fertility rate of the Indigenous population from 2006 to 2011, compared to a 5.2% increase in the non-Indigenous population (Statistics Canada, 2016a).

Composing 4.9% of the total Canadian population in 2016, Indigenous People have experienced significant growth in the population within the past decade (42.5%) and an 18.9% growth rate in the past five years (Statistics Canada, 2017d). Furthermore, Canada's Indigenous population is very young in comparison with age distributions of non-Indigenous Canadians. Nearly half (46.2%) of the Indigenous population in 2011 was 24 years old or less compared to only 29.5% of the non-Indigenous population (Statistics

Canada, 2011c; Aboriginal Affairs and Northern Development Canada, 2013). In 2016, the average age of an Indigenous person (32.1 years old) was nearly a decade younger than the average age of a non-Indigenous person (40 years) (Statistics Canada, 2017d).

Previous work by the OECD highlights how an estimated 350 000 Indigenous youth will turn 15 years old between 2016-26, which provides an unprecedented opportunity to leverage investments in job and skills training and employment readiness for Indigenous youth in order to fill crucial labour shortages in Canada (OECD, 2016).

Figure 1.1. Age Distribution for Canadian Indigenous and non-Indigenous Populations, 2016

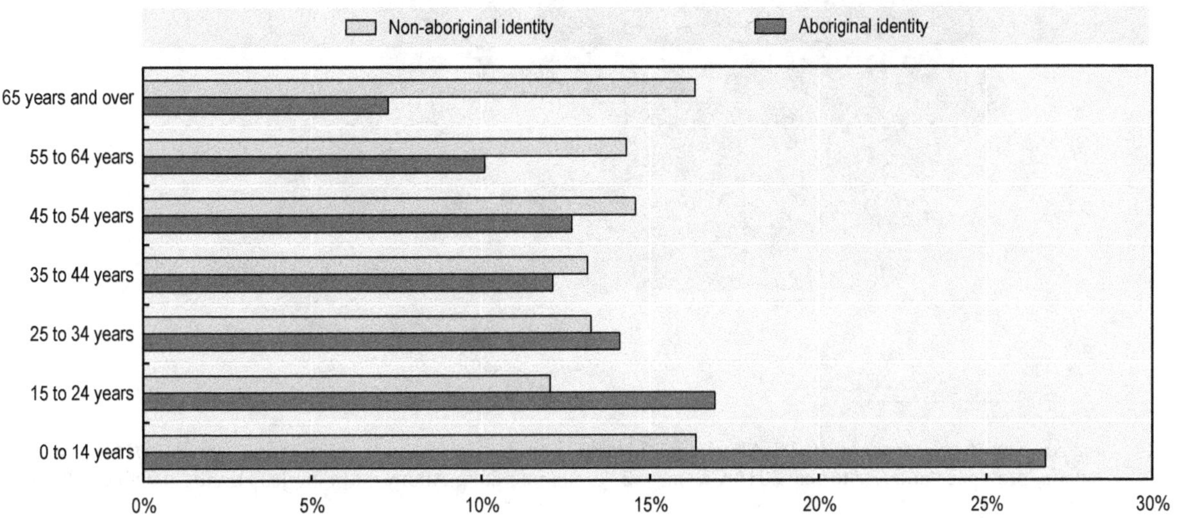

Source: Statistics Canada (2017), *Aboriginal identity population by age and sex*, Catalogue no. 98-402-X2016009, National Household Survey 2016, available at http://www12.statcan.gc.ca/census-recensement/2016/dp-pd/hlt-fst/abo-aut/index-eng.cfm.

StatLink http://dx.doi.org/10.1787/888933723739

Geographic residency of Indigenous People

Figure 1.2 shows geographic locations of Indigenous People across Canada's provinces and territories in 2016. Data from the 2006 Census to the 2016 Census illustrates trends in Indigenous People migrating from rural to urban settings. During that time, the population of Indigenous People living in metropolitan areas increased by 59.7%. Therefore, more than half (51.8%) of the Indigenous Population live in metropolitan centres in Canada as of 2016 (Statistics Canada, 2017).

In 2016, the province with the highest number of Indigenous People was Ontario (374 395 people), which was a 54.1 percentage change over the past five years. With one-fifth of the total Métis population, Ontario had the largest Métis population in Canada (120 585) in 2016. This was a 64.3% from the population in 2006 (Statistics Canada, 2017).

In comparison, over the past decade, there was a 75.1% growth from in the population of First Nations which did not have registered or treaty Indian status (232 375 people) and a 30.8% growth in First Nations who have registered or treaty Indian status (744 855 people). First Nations with registered or treaty Indian status therefore accounted for 76.2% of the First Nations population (Statistics Canada, 2017).

Figure 1.2. Percentage of Indigenous populations per Canadian province, 2016

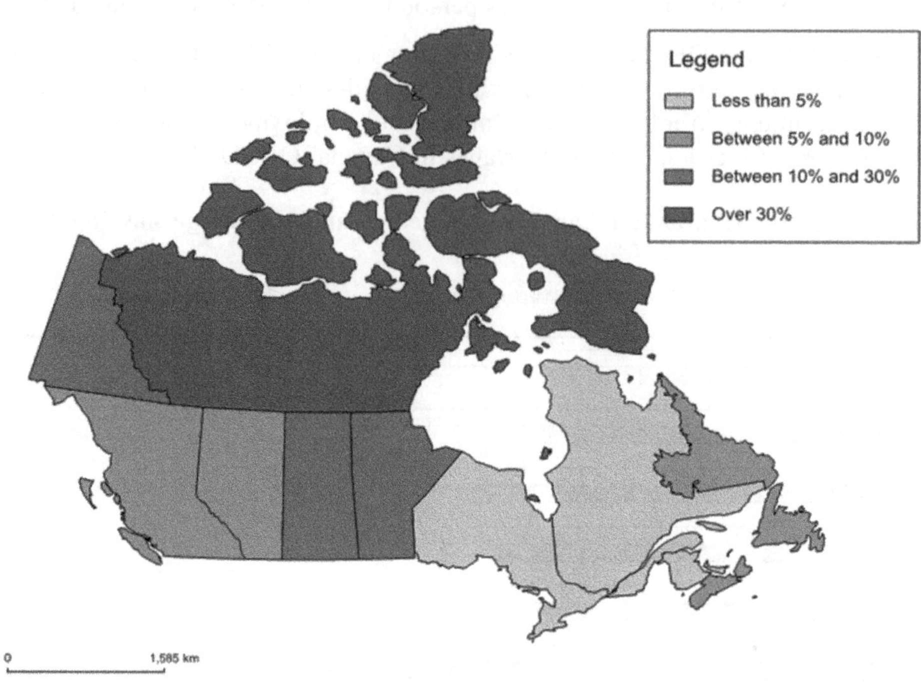

Source: Statistics Canada (2017), Aboriginal identity population by both sexes, total - age, 2016 counts, Canada, provinces and territories, 2016 Census – 25% Sample data, Aboriginal Peoples Highlight Tables, 2016 Census, http://www12.statcan.gc.ca/census-recensement/2016/dp-pd/hlt-fst/abo-aut/Table.cfm?Lang=Eng&T=101&D1=1&D2=1&D3=1&RPP=25&PR=0&SR=1&S=102&O=D (accessed on 25 January 2018).

StatLink http://dx.doi.org/10.1787/888933723758

Indigenous identity

The data which refers to the Indigenous population in this report only includes the population which selected to be recognised as having an "Aboriginal Identity" in the Canadian Census. Because Indigenous history, culture and identity are complex concepts, the census also asks whether the respondent has "Aboriginal Heritage". Compared to the 1.7 million people who reported "Aboriginal Identities" in 2011, 2.1 million Canadians recorded an Aboriginal ancestry in the 2016 Census (Statistics Canada, 2016a). This means that about 400 000 respondents are decedents of Aboriginal ancestors, but did not identify on the census as Indigenous. Canada allows citizens to self-identify as Indigenous since the identity of Indigenous People are nuanced in every form—both individually and collectively. By giving Canadians the autonomy to choose if they identify as Indigenous, the government recognises that each individual has the legitimacy to determine their own identity (Indigenous and Northern Affairs Canada, 2013). While the government enables individuals to self-identify as Indigenous, this is different than Indian Status, which is determined under the *Indian Act*. Under the *Indian Act*, Status Indians, also known as registered Indians, may be eligible for a range of benefits, rights, programmes and services offered by the federal and provincial or territorial governments.

It is also important to note that the Canadian constitution recognises three groups of Indigenous People: Indians (commonly referred to as First Nation), Inuit and Métis.

Within the Census, Indigenous People are distinguished as Registered Indian, Métis, Non-Status Indian, Inuit and other Aboriginal (respondents who identify with more than one Indigenous group or as a Band member with no Aboriginal identity and no Registered Indian Status) (Indigenous and Northern Affairs Canada, 2013).

Measuring labour market outcomes

In 2016, Canada's total population observed a 7% unemployment rate with 7.7% of men and 6.2% of women unemployed. This number has steadily decreased since its highest point in the past decade—a rate of 8.4% unemployment in 2009. As of December 2017, unemployment continued its downward trend sitting at 5.9%—the lowest rate since February 2008 (Statistics Canada, 2016g; OECD, 2017a; OECD, 2017b).

Despite these favourable labour market conditions, Indigenous and non-Indigenous Canadians do not share the same labour market outcomes and the differences between the two groups are striking along many indicators. While in general, Indigenous Canadians have fallen behind in labour market performance, some indicators show varying outcomes across regions.

In Figure 1.3, data from the 2016 Census shows that on average across Canada, non-Indigenous People have higher labour market participation rates[1] than Indigenous People. The gaps between outcomes of the two groups are particularly wide in Nunavut, Northwest Territories, Saskatchewan, and Manitoba with differences of 29.3%, 20.7%, 13.2% and 10.5% respectively (Statistics Canada, 2016f).

Figure 1.3. Gaps in Participation Rate Percentages

Canadian Provinces and Territories, Indigenous Status, Ages 15 years and older, 2016

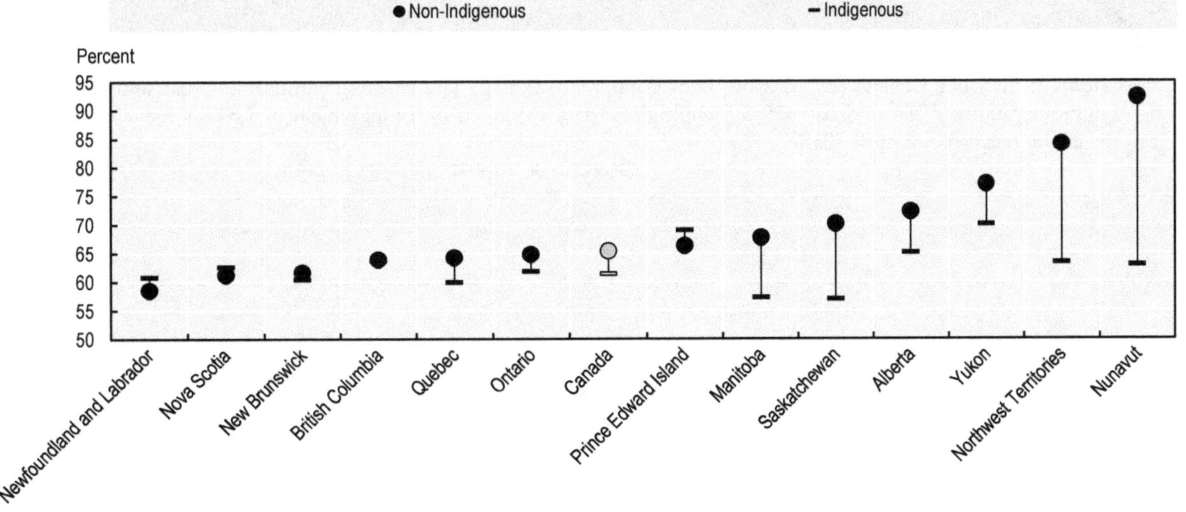

Source: Statistics Canada (2016) Census of Population. Canada and census metropolitan areas and census agglomerations, 2016 Census – 25% Sample data, data extracted by Employment and Skills Development Canada, received 11 April 2018.

StatLink http://dx.doi.org/10.1787/888933723777

Labour market outcomes across provinces

In regards to employment rates[2], Nunavut, Northwest Territories, Saskatchewan and Yukon have the greatest gaps in performances between Indigenous and non-Indigenous groups with differences of 43.8%, 29%, 19.9% and 18.1%, respectively. These trends are illustrated in Figure 1.4, showing that Newfoundland and Labrador and Nova Scotia have the smallest outcome gaps. However, they are also among the provinces and territories with the lowest employment rates (Statistics Canada, 2016f).

Figure 1.5 illustrates unemployment rate gaps across all Canadian provinces for 2016. The unemployment rate was particularly high for the Indigenous population in the territories and Atlantic region. The differences in unemployment rate percentages between Indigenous and non-Indigenous groups are highest in Nunavut (24.6%), Yukon (16.3%), and Northwest Territories (14.5%) (Statistics Canada, 2016f).

Figure 1.4. Gaps in Employment Rate Percentages

Canadian Provinces, Indigenous Status, Ages 15 years and older, 2016

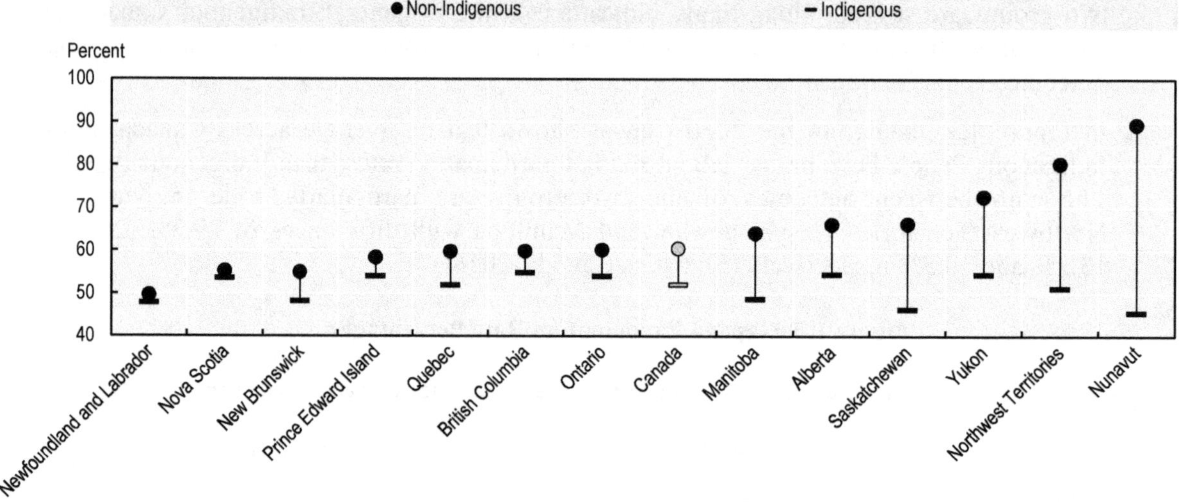

Source: Statistics Canada (2016), Census of Population. Canada and census metropolitan areas and census agglomerations, 2016 Census – 25% Sample data, data extracted by Employment and Skills Development Canada, received 11 April 2018.

StatLink http://dx.doi.org/10.1787/888933723796

Figure 1.5. Gaps in Unemployment Rate Percentages

Canadian Provinces, Indigenous Status, Ages 15 years and older, 2016

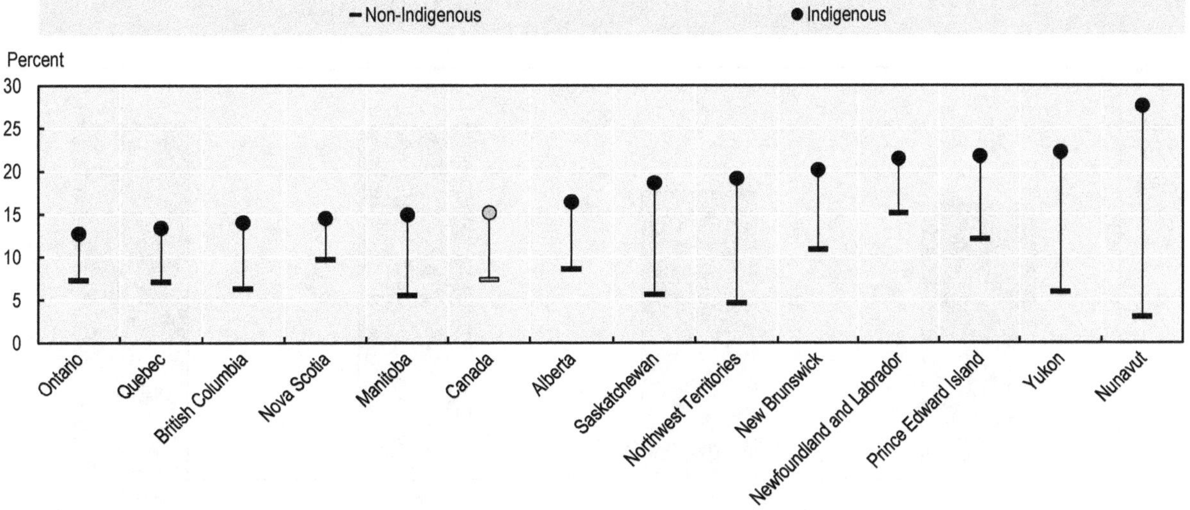

Source: Statistics Canada (2016), Census of Population. Canada and census metropolitan areas and census agglomerations, 2016 Census – 25% Sample data, data extracted by Employment and Skills Development Canada, received 11 April 2018.

StatLink http://dx.doi.org/10.1787/888933723815

Trends in labour market indicators across Indigenous groups

Similar to geographic trends, labour market outcomes can vary between Indigenous groups. Figure 1.6 illustrates how different Indigenous groups performed in the 2016 Census regarding employment rates and the percent of the population outside of the labour force. As expected, each indicator has an inverse relationship. Also, each group performs consistently. However, the amount of each population employed is quite low and the percent of the population not in the labour force is rather high (especially for the groups with the worst outcomes in each indicator). Finally, of the Indigenous groups, the outcomes of the Métis are closest to those of Non-Indigenous People. This is considerably higher than First Nations and Inuit populations (Statistics Canada, 2016f).

Figure 1.6. Labour Market Outcomes by Indigenous Group

Canada, Ages 15 years and older, 2016

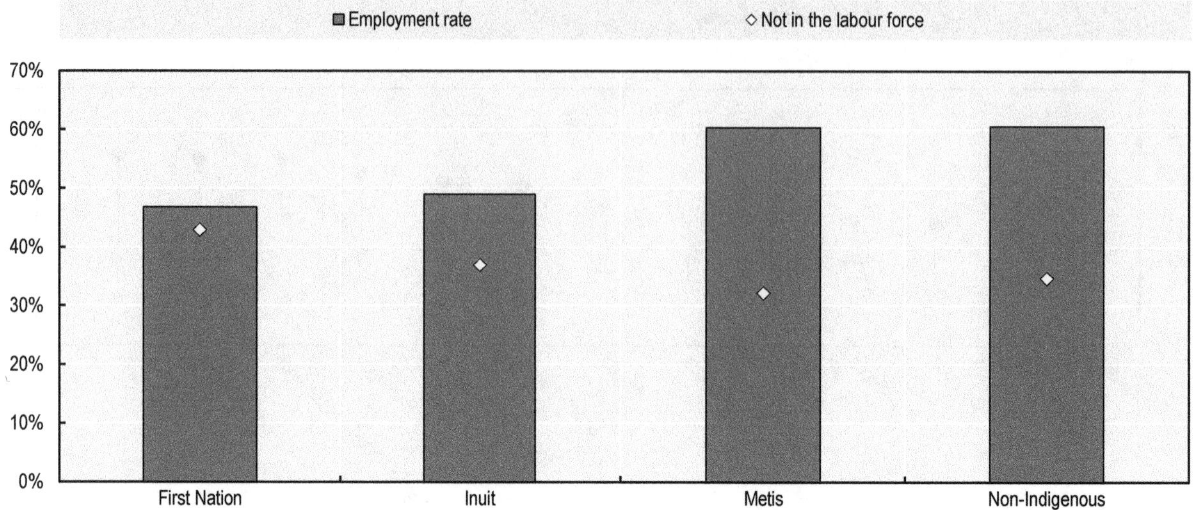

Source: Statistics Canada (2016), Census of Population. Canada and census metropolitan areas and census agglomerations, 2016 Census – 25% Sample data, data extracted by Employment and Skills Development Canada, received 11 April 2018.

StatLink http://dx.doi.org/10.1787/888933723834

Trends in Indigenous status and gender outcomes over the last decade[3]

In the past decade, Indigenous groups have almost always experienced worse outcomes within participation rates, employment rates and unemployment rates than their non-Indigenous counterparts. However, Indigenous females had consistently observed the lowest outcomes when looking at the labour market participation rate and employment rate. Within unemployment rates, Indigenous men consistently had the worst performance.

Indigenous women's outcomes tend to be slightly improving while Indigenous men's outcomes are slowly worsening. Also, note that the global financial crisis of 2008 shook labour market outcomes in 2009 and 2010. But what is most striking is that non-Indigenous were far less effected by the crisis. The outcomes of Indigenous People can partially be explained by their younger age, since youth are more at risk to unemployment (especially during downturns). Additionally, Indigenous People are underrepresented in knowledge industries and overrepresented in industries that were more affected by the financial crisis, like construction (see Figure 1.12).

Figure 1.7. Trends in Gender within Participation Rate Percentages for the Years 2007-2016

Canada, Indigenous Status, Sex, Ages 15-64

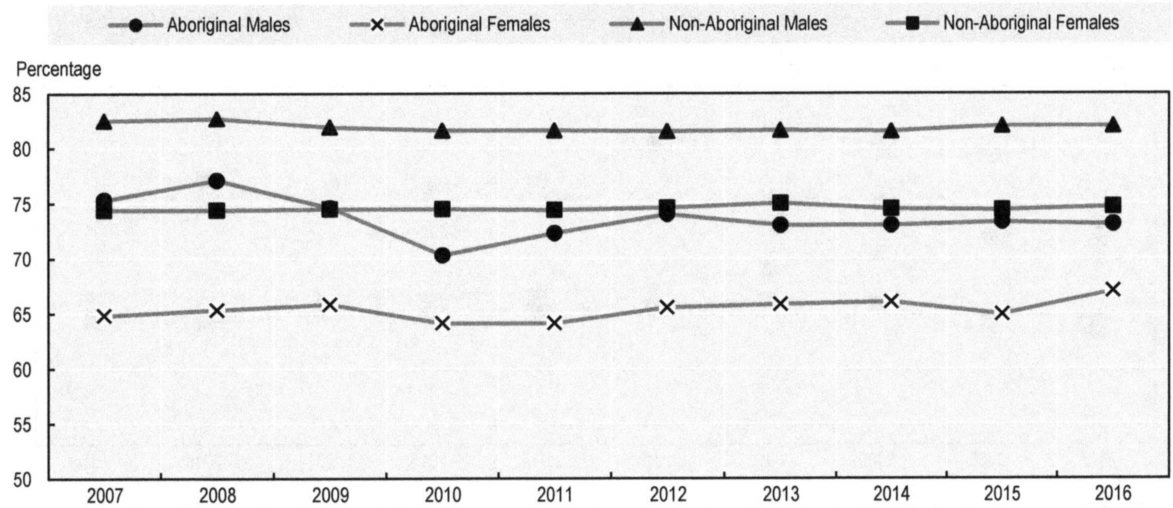

Note: Excluded from the survey's coverage are persons living on reserves and other Aboriginal settlements in the provinces as well as those living in the territories.
Source: Statistics Canada. Table 282-0226- Labour force survey estimates (LFS), by Aboriginal group, sex and age group, Canada, selected provinces and regions, annual (persons), CANSIM (database), (accessed on 3 July 2017).

StatLink http://dx.doi.org/10.1787/888933723853

Figure 1.8. Trends in Gender within Employment Rate Percentages for the Years 2007-2016

Canada, Indigenous Status, Sex, Ages 15-64

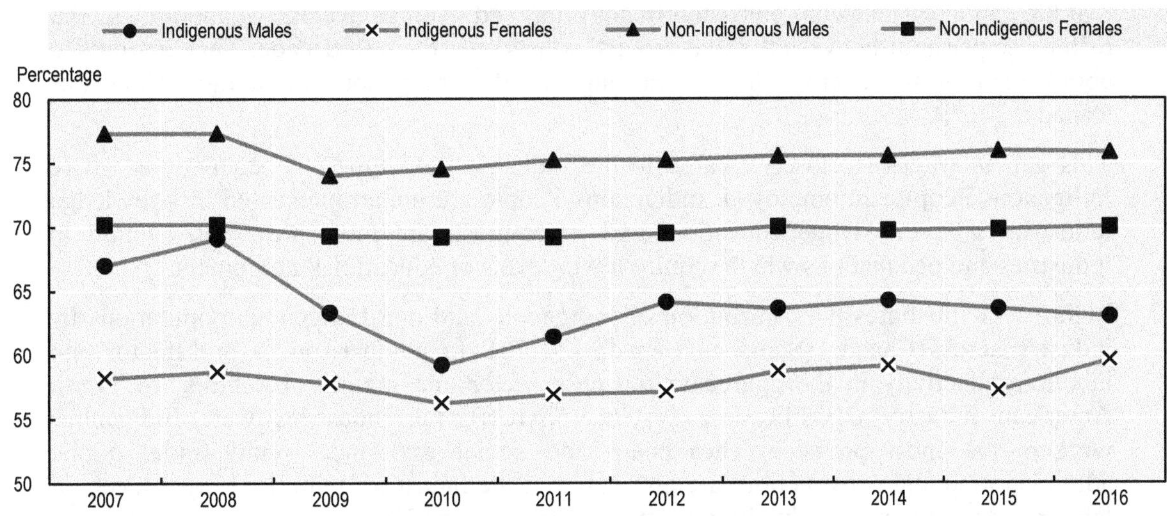

Note: Excluded from the survey's coverage are persons living on reserves and other Aboriginal settlements in the provinces as well as those living in the territories.
Source: Statistics Canada. Table 282-0226- Labour force survey estimates (LFS), by Aboriginal group, sex and age group, Canada, selected provinces and regions, annual (persons), CANSIM (database), (accessed on 3 July 2017).

StatLink http://dx.doi.org/10.1787/888933723872

Figure 1.9. Trends in Gender within Unemployment Rate Percentages for the Years 2007-2016

Canada, Indigenous Status, Sex, Ages 15-64

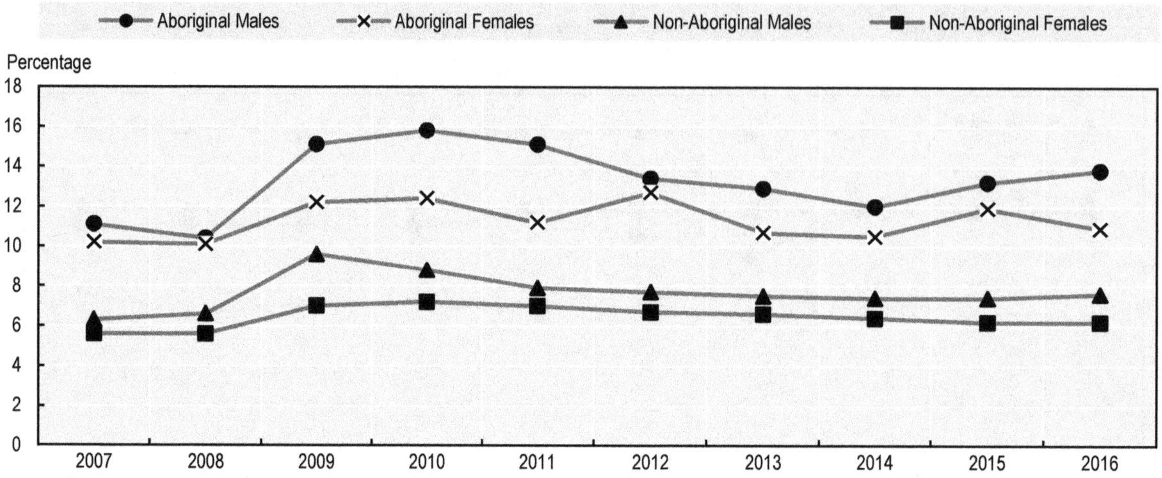

Note: Excluded from the survey's coverage are persons living on reserves and other Aboriginal settlements in the provinces as well as those living in the territories.

Source: Statistics Canada. Table 282-0226- Labour force survey estimates (LFS), by Aboriginal group, sex and age group, Canada, selected provinces and regions, annual (persons), CANSIM (database), (accessed on 3 July 2017).

StatLink http://dx.doi.org/10.1787/888933723891

Wage, industry and occupation gaps

While barriers to employment for Indigenous People still need to be reduced, those who participate in the labour force have consistently experienced disparities in wages and income. Figure 1.10 illustrates trends in wages over the past decade. This demonstrates that the gap in earnings has consistently not improved, with an average of about CAD 2.5 difference per hour between the two groups' wages over the past decade. That amounts to about 11% of the average hourly earnings of the Indigenous population (Statistics Canada, 2017j).

This gap in wages is closely related to the industries and types of occupations where Indigenous People are employed. Indigenous People are underrepresented in knowledge industries and knowledge education, and in contrast, are most prevalently found in industries and occupations which require lower levels of educational attainment.

Figure 1.11 illustrates the distribution of Indigenous and non-Indigenous populations by industry across Canada (Statistics Canada, 2011b). In comparison to multifactor and labour productivity in the aggregate business sector and major sub-sectors, by North American Industry Classification System (NAICS), the industries were Indigenous workers are most prevalent (healthcare and social assistance, retail trade, public administration and construction) are also some of the industries with the lowest levels of labour and multifactor productivity (Statistics Canada, 2017f).

Along with trends seen within knowledge-based industry, Indigenous People are also less commonly found knowledge worker occupations. This is closely connected to disparities in educational outcomes between Indigenous and non-Indigenous students. Figure 1.12 shows that Indigenous workers are found more prevalently in occupations requiring lower educational attainment in comparison to non-Indigenous workers (Statistics Canada, 2011b).

Figure 1.10. Average hourly wages for Indigenous and non-Indigenous identity populations, constant prices, Canada and selected provinces, 2007-2016

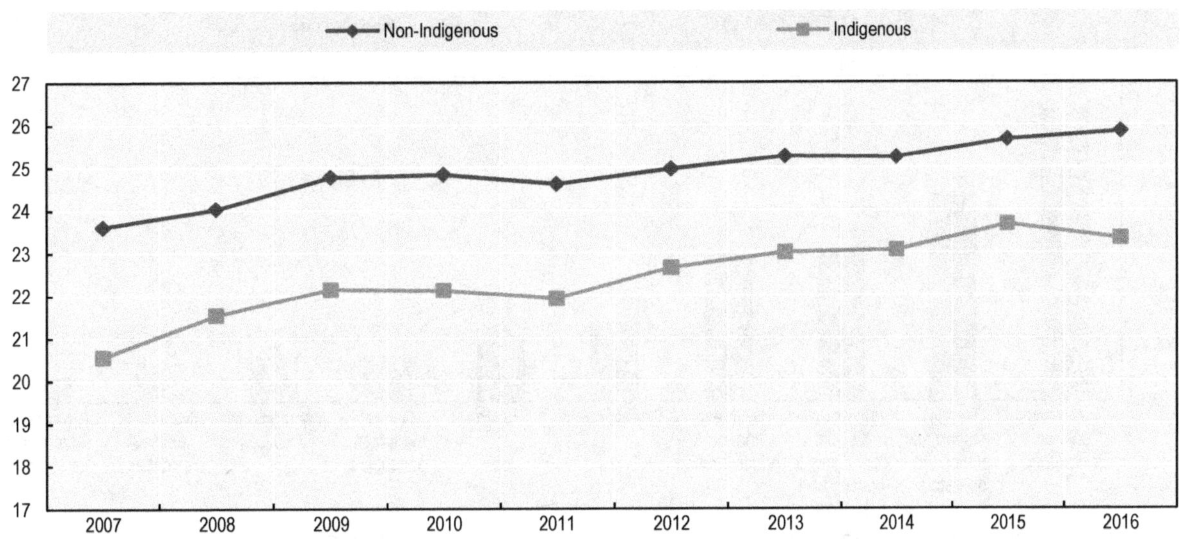

Source: Statistics Canada (2017). Table 282-0233 - Labour force survey estimates (LFS), average hourly and weekly wages and average usual weekly hours by Aboriginal group and age group, Canada, selected provinces and regions, 2007-2016.

StatLink http://dx.doi.org/10.1787/888933723910

Figure 1.11. Employment distribution of the Indigenous and non-Indigenous identity populations by industry, 15 and older, %, 2016

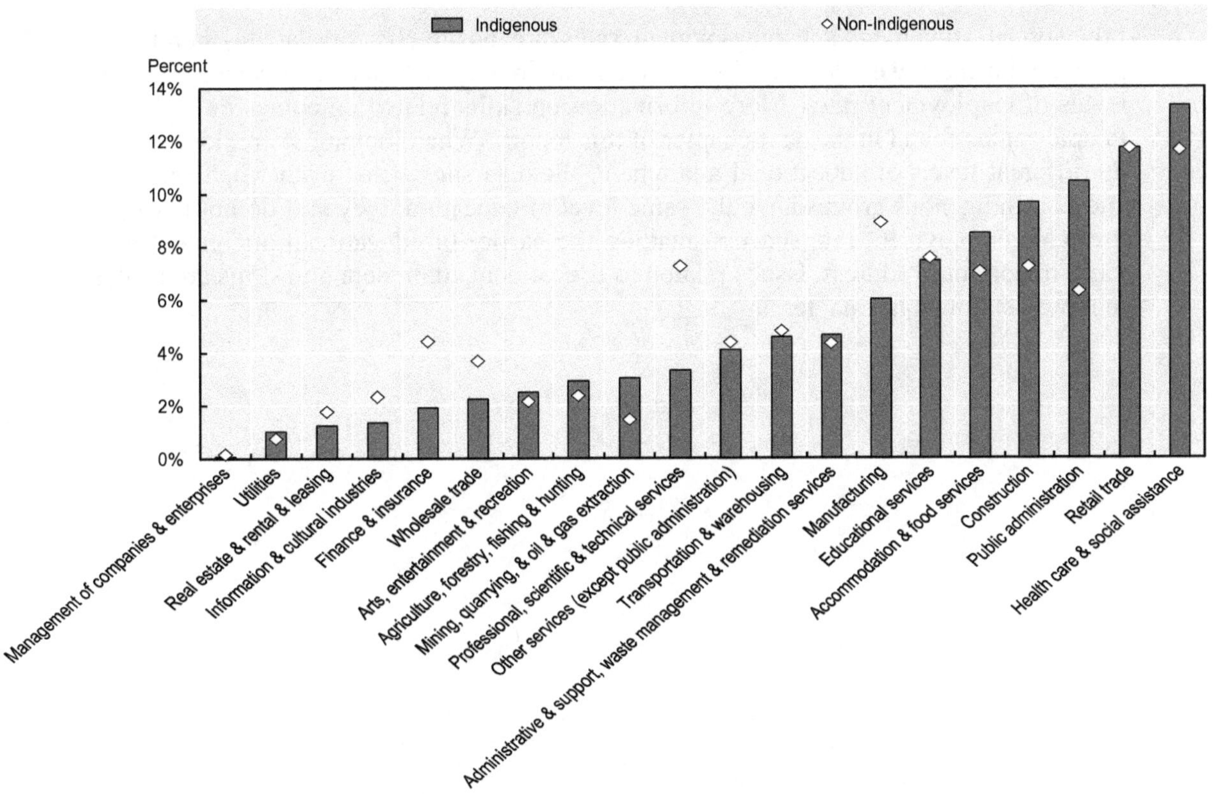

Source: Statistics Canada (2016), 2016 Census, Catalogue no. 98-400-X2016359.

StatLink http://dx.doi.org/10.1787/888933723929

Figure 1.12. Employment distribution of the Indigenous and non-Indigenous identity populations by occupation, 15 and older, %, 2016

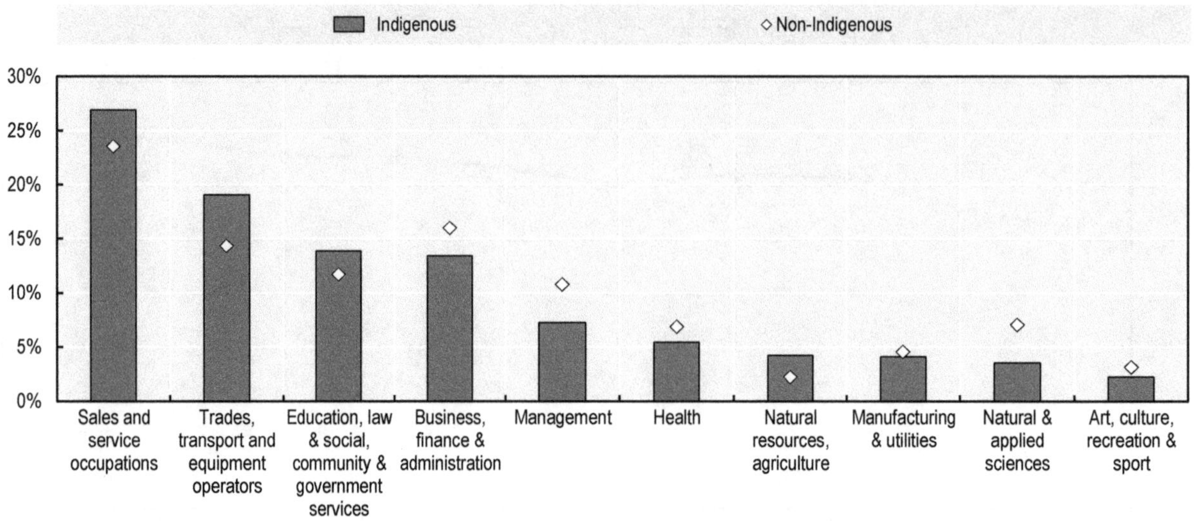

Indigenous ◇ Non-Indigenous

30% 25% 20% 15% 10% 5% 0%

Sales and service occupations | Trades, transport and equipment operators | Education, law & social, community & government services | Business, finance & administration | Management | Health | Natural resources, agriculture | Manufacturing & utilities | Natural & applied sciences | Art, culture, recreation & sport

Source : Statistics Canada (2016), 2016 Census, Catalogue no. 98-400-X2016357.

StatLink http://dx.doi.org/10.1787/888933723948

What are the barriers to employment for Indigenous People?

Educational attainment

Educational attainment and employment rates are positively correlated—therefore the people with the lowest levels of educational attainment will also experience the lowest levels of employment rates. More information on skills related outcomes on Indigenous People can be found in the next chapter of this report. When looking at employment rates by different levels of educational attainment, the data shows that even when Indigenous and non-Indigenous groups have the same level of education, they still do not experience the same employment rate success, making the barrier of educational attainment all the more important to address. Issues related to educational attainment and skills are analysed in more detail within Chapter 5.

Figure 1.13 Employment rate of population aged 25 to 64, by highest level of educational attainment, Indigenous identity, Canada, 2016

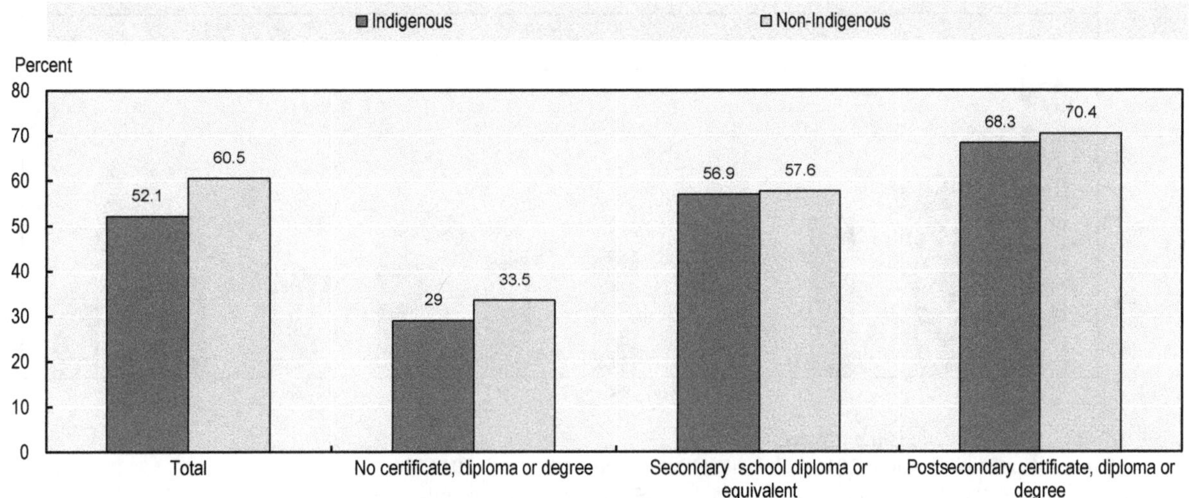

Source: Statistics Canada (2016), Census of Population, Statistics Canada Catalogue no. 98-400-X2016265.

StatLink http://dx.doi.org/10.1787/888933723967

The 2012 Aboriginal Peoples Survey (APS) asked unemployed Indigenous People what they found was the most prevalent reason(s) for not obtaining work. The survey compared the responses of those who did not obtain a high school diploma and those who did. A lack of education or training was the highest reported reason for Indigenous People without high school diplomas in all Indigenous groups except for Inuit People, who reported a shortage of work as the highest reason. The gaps between those with and without high school diplomas were highest for this reason as well (Statistics Canada, 2015).

Socio-economic Status (SES)

Figure 1.14 illustrates the disproportionate representation of Indigenous People in lower income groups in 2016. In comparison, non-Indigenous People are proportionately disbursed in all income deciles, with an average of 10% of non-Indigenous People in each decile (Statistics Canada, 2016e). Additionally, according to Statistics Canada a prevalence of low income was found within 23% of the Indigenous population compared to 13.8% of the non-Indigenous population in 2016 (Statistics Canada, 2016e).

Figure 1.14. Percentage of Indigenous People in each income decile group (after-tax), 2016

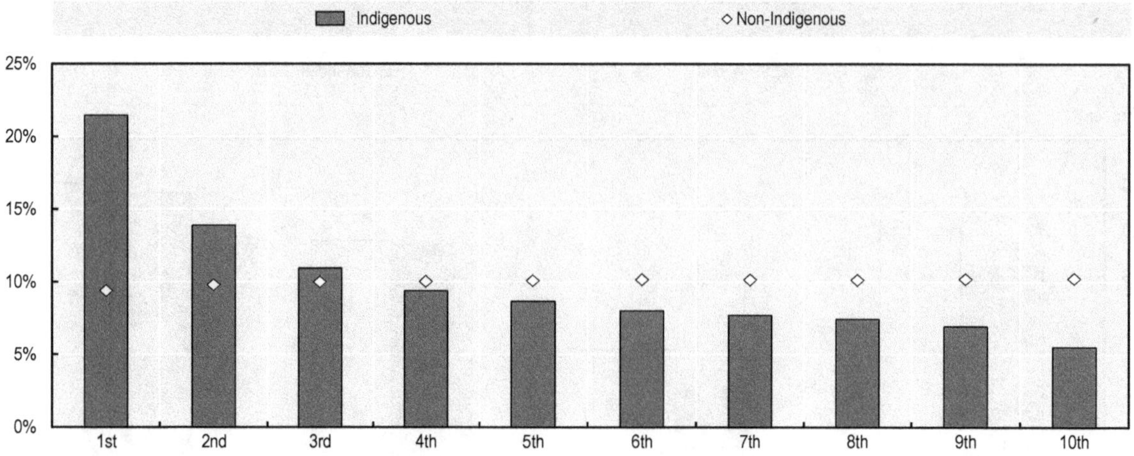

Indigenous
◇ Non-Indigenous
25%
20%
15%
10%
5%
0%
1st 2nd 3rd 4th 5th 6th 7th 8th 9th 10th

Note: The 10th decile is the top decile.
Source: Statistics Canada (2016), Census, Catalogue no. 98-400-X2016174.
StatLink http://dx.doi.org/10.1787/888933723986

Disproportionate levels of incarceration and policing

Indigenous People are incarcerated at a disproportionate rate in comparison to the general population. Considering the projected growth rate of the Indigenous population in Canada, this means that there could be growing numbers of Indigenous People re-entering society with a criminal record, which places pressure on inclusive growth and social cohesion if they are not able to find a job (Statistics Canada, 2015). In this context, it would be important to consider ways to support this particular group of individuals.

Figure 1.15. Indigenous and non-Indigenous adult correctional services, custodial admissions to provincial and territorial programmes by Indigenous identity, annual (number), 2000-2016

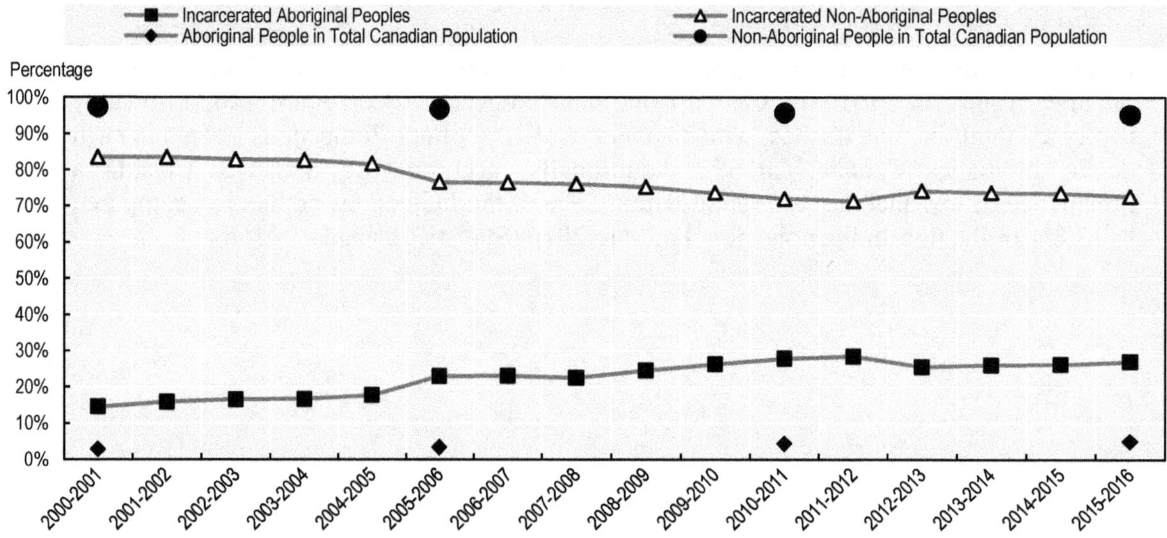

Note: In the Northwest Territories, other custodial status admissions data as of 2007/2008 are not available.
Source: Statistics Canada. Table 251-0022 - Adult correctional services, custodial admissions to provincial and territorial programs by Aboriginal identity, annual (number), CANSIM (database) (accessed: 3 July 2017).
StatLink http://dx.doi.org/10.1787/888933724005

Federal policies and programmes supporting Indigenous employment outcomes

In his speech at the 9th Session of the United Nations Permanent Forum on Indigenous Issues, TRC Chair the Honourable Justice Murray Sinclair emphasised that Residential Schools in Canada lasted over 150 years, with the last school closing in 1996, equating to about seven generations of school attendance. He recognized while healing will take time, the Canadian government cannot delay its efforts to start achieving reconciliation. Urged by the TRC's Call to Actions, the Canadian government has sought to prioritise Indigenous rights and illuminate the importance of acting now (Sinclair, 2016). At the federal level, a number of programmes and policies have been introduced to aid the reconciliation process and are creating successful narratives for Indigenous People, often managed and delivered by Indigenous communities themselves.

From a labour market perspective, the key actor is Employment and Social Development Canada (ESDC). As a federal body, ESDC strives to foster a dynamic, skilled and diverse workforce. This is manifested through its work on employment and skills policies. ESDC also provides skills training programmes to encourage inclusive workforce participation and lifelong learning.

At the federal level, another key partner implementing policies and programmes benefiting Indigenous People is Indigenous and Northern Affairs Canada (INAC). In August 2017, the dissolution of INAC was announced which has resulted in the creation of two new departments: Indigenous Services Canada and Crown-Indigenous Relations and Northern Affairs Canada. INAC acts as the federal department for the management of economic development policies for Indigenous People. The management of economic development policies is composed of the following policy and programme areas: Indigenous Entrepreneurship, Community Economic Development, Strategic Partnerships, Infrastructure and Capacity, and Urban Indigenous Participation.

Indigenous Skills and Employment Training Strategy

The Indigenous Skills and Employment Training Strategy (ISETS) [4], established in 2010 by Employment and Social Development Canada, includes funding of 292 million CAD annually and 10 year funding agreements. ISETS is a broad-based, foundational labour market programme that provides a full suite of skills development and job training, from the acquisition of essential skills, such as literacy and numeracy, to more advanced training for in-demand jobs. Built on a succession of programmes since 1991, ISETS includes the three strategic pillars of demand-driven training, partnerships and accountability for results (Employment and Social Development Canada, 2017).

ISETS supports a network of 85 Indigenous service delivery organisations that design and deliver employment programmes and services for Indigenous People with over 600 points of service across Canada. All Indigenous People, regardless of status or location, may access its programmes and services. ISETS interventions include: job-finding skills and training, wage subsidies to encourage employers to hire Indigenous workers, financial subsidies to help individuals access employment or obtain skills for employment, entrepreneurial skills development, supports to help with returning to school, and child care for parents in training (Employment and Social Development Canada, 2017).

An additional CAD 50 million was allocated to ISETS in both 2016-17 and 2017-18 through a combination of new funding and reallocated resources. This funding was used to support communities at risk and literacy and essential skills, fund 15 pilot projects to better align training with community needs in the areas of housing construction, water treatment, child care and local administration as well as strengthen capacity across the network of service providers to meet the growing demand from Indigenous People for skills development and job training.

In preparation for programme renewal, the Government proposed through Budget 2016, to consult with Indigenous partners to inform the future of Indigenous labour market programming. The Minister of Employment, Workforce Development and Labour (EWDL) and Senior Officials undertook extensive engagement with National Indigenous Organisations; Indigenous leadership; ISETS agreement holders; provinces and territories; industry; and academic institutions, to gather their views on the strengthens and weaknesses of the current programming, to ensure future Indigenous labour market programming meets the needs of Indigenous People.

In addition, Indigenous partners were encouraged to submit completed discussion guides or comments along with any other relevant material or resources to ESDC to help inform the future of Indigenous labour market programming.

Since 2011-2012, over 367,000 Indigenous People have participated in the ISETS program, of which over 121,000 individuals have become employed, and over 59,000 have returned to school. Furthermore, since 2011-2012, more than 13 000 Indigenous People have participated in wage subsidy programs and approximately 3,200 people have accessed childcare through the ISETS. Approximately 1,700 ISETS clients have participated in one or more self-employment interventions and have become self-employed following their participation.

The federal government's Budget 2018 announced new investments of CAD 2 billion over five years, and CAD 408.2 million per year ongoing, to support the Indigenous Skills and Employment Training (ISET) Programme,. This includes incremental investments of CAD 447 million over five years, and CAD 99.4 million per year ongoing, designed as 10 year funding agreements and a stronger focus on training for higher-quality, better-paying jobs rather than rapid re-employment. Recognising the importance of a distinctions-based approach, the programme will support the creation of four labour market streams for First Nations, Inuit, Metis and urban/non-affiliated Indigenous People. The Department is planning a distinctions-based engagement with Indigenous partners to co-develop the implementation of the new ISET Programme features in 2018-19.

Accountability provisions

The objective of ISET is to increase Indigenous participation in the Canadian labour market, ensuring that First Nations, Métis and Inuit people are engaged in sustainable, meaningful employment. The objective supports the Government of Canada's overarching goals of promoting skills development, labour market participation and inclusiveness and ensuring labour market efficiency.

Currently, the agreement holders under ISET would receive a five-year commitment to undertake programming. Progress toward the goals and objectives of the initiative is measured through direct, intermediate and ultimate outcomes as established in the Performance Measurement Strategy. Examples of the key performance measurement indicators include:

- Number of clients served by type of intervention;
- Number of clients who successfully complete interventions as planned;
- Number of clients who returned to school following completion of intervention(s), and
- Number of clients employed following completion of intervention(s).

The Strategic Partnerships Initiative

Established in 2010, the Strategic Partnerships Initiative (SPI) continues to be innovative in addressing Indigenous economic development through its governance, decision making process and investments. As part of INAC's Lands and Economic Development (LED) Sector's vision to restore Indigenous People land base, control and access their lands and resources, freely pursue wealth creation and share fully in Canada's prosperity, SPI is a key cross-governmental horizontal mechanism to increase Indigenous participation in complex multi-year economic opportunities. SPI coordinates the efforts and investments of multiple federal partners, which includes a focus on supporting Indigenous community economic readiness and participation in complex economic opportunities across Canada. The role of economic development and job creation are among LED and SPI's goals, which includes closing the socio-economic gaps, greater self-determination and improved relations.

The SPI, as a horizontal mechanism, coordinates multiple federal department investments focused on Indigenous economic development as well as streamline administrative processes to ensure a whole of government and one-window approach. The SPI recipients include other levels of government, tribal councils, self-governing First Nations, Indigenous communities, businesses, partnerships and joint ventures.

For instance, in the Ontario's Ring of Fire region, SPI is supporting the Community Wellbeing Pilot Project with Neskantaga, Webequie, and Marten Falls First Nations in partnership with the Matawa Tribal Council, provincial ministries and federal departments. Using a holistic, place-based approach to community development, the project is challenging governments to go beyond their role as funders and become developmental partners in addressing community-identified needs and priorities. To date, significant progress is being made in the areas of housing, skills and training, financial management and governance, and mental health and additions. Addressing these core social challenges ensures that communities are better able to prepare for and benefit from mineral and economic development opportunities in their traditional territories.

Indigenous policies and programmes within provinces and territories

Provinces and territories in Canada also play a critical role in working with Indigenous communities to reduce inequalities. In most cases, each province and territory has a dedicated Minister responsible for improving the economic and social outcomes of Indigenous People. Furthermore, in many cases, provinces would allocate additional funding to Indigenous programmes.

Through federally-funded labour market transfer agreements, provinces and territories design and deliver their own suite of labour market and skills programmes for unemployed and underemployed Canadians, including Indigenous and non-Indigenous people (OECD, 2014). While not specific to Indigenous People, they would still access services through these programmes depending on eligibility criteria established by the province.

The largest labour market transfer agreements are the Labour Market Development Agreements (LMDAs) which provide unemployed Canadians, mainly eligible under Employment Insurance, with skills training and employment supports to help them find and maintain employment. Measures available include skills training, wage subsidies, self-employment supports, and work experience opportunities. LMDAs also provide employment assistance services (e.g. job search assistance, employment counselling) for all unemployed Canadians. Under Budget 2017, the Government expanded the LMDAs and broadened eligibility for programs and services to help more Canadians, including under-represented groups, access EI-funded skills training and employment supports. Additional flexibility was also introduced to expand employment assistance services to employed workers and to support employer-sponsored training.

In addition to the LMDAs, the federal government's Budget 2017 announced the creation of new Workforce Development Agreements (WDAs), which consolidate the existing Canada Job Fund Agreements, the Labour Market Agreements for Persons with Disabilities and the Targeted Initiative for Older Workers, making transfers to the provinces and territories simpler and more flexible to ensure programming meets local labour market needs. Under the WDAs, provinces and territories provide skills training and employment supports to non-EI eligible, unemployed, or underemployed Canadians, including those further removed from the labour market, and employers.

Inter-governmental bodies for policy co-operation and coordination

Forum of Labour Market Ministers

The Forum of Labour Market Ministers (FLMM) was created in 1983 to promote discussion and co-operation on labour market matters. The forum is composed of federal, provincial and territorial (FPT) government departments that work collaboratively to address common labour market goals and issues in Canada. It informs FPT programmes and policies, as well as numerous stakeholders. As the climate of the Canadian labour market continually shifts, the Forum addresses both persistent and emerging labour market issues.

The FLMM is co-chaired by the Minister of Employment, Workforce Development and Labour at the ESDC and a lead province. The Forum's governance model includes Ministers', Deputy Ministers', and Senior Officials' tables, as well as working groups for ongoing business. The Forum's Secretariat, hosted by the provincial/territorial Co-Chair, supports the Forum and coordinates activities to advance the common priorities set by FPT ministers responsible for labour market issues. It is a neutral body that is responsible for facilitating provincial/territorial collaboration and consensus, and ensuring a coherent vision that is fully representative of all governments. Five overarching objectives for the FLMM include:

- Ensuring the next generation of Labour Market Transfer Agreements (LMTAs) are client-centred, outcomes focused, inclusive flexible and responsive, and evidence-based to meet the needs of Canadian workers and employers;
- Optimising the integration of internationally-trained workers and the mobility of certified workers and apprentices to meet industry and labour market needs;
- Promoting demand-led training, as well as employer involvement to respond to labour market demands and support increased productivity;
- Strengthening strategic planning capacity to better respond to Canada's changing labour market needs through engaging partners, knowledge development and the effective use of labour market information, and
- Promoting sharing of best practices to advance labour market issues and support efforts to increase labour market policy and programming innovation in Canada.

New FPT Working Groups have been created to implement the Strategic Plan, Chaired by both a representative from the federal government and a province, or territory, each has developed annual work plans. The current working groups are: LMTAs & Performance Measurement Working Group; Labour Market Information Council Implementation Support Committee; Strategic Foresight and Engagement Working Group; Innovation and Best Practices Working Group; and Mobility and Qualification Recognition Working Group. The Strategic Foresight and Engagement Working Group is the Forum's focal point for collaboration and engagement with key partners and stakeholders such as Indigenous organisations, employers and labour market experts.

Labour Market Management Committees

The Labour Market Management Committees (LMMC's) governance structure supports bilateral strategic discussions on labour market issues and priorities between ESDC and provinces/territories. The LMMC's governance structure was established to oversee the implementation and management of LMTAs between the federal government and provinces/territories. These bilateral meetings provide a forum for strategic discussions of labour market issues and priorities, support the federal government and provincial/territorial governments in fulfilling their respective obligations under the agreements, and foster coordinated and integrated approaches to support policy and programme effectiveness as well as administrative and operational efficiencies.

The federal government is looking to leverage existing intergovernmental fora on labour market issues, including the Forum of Labour Market Ministers and the Labour Market Management Committees, to continue working with provinces and territories to ensure greater program complementarities including identifying approach for increased coordination of Federal-Provincial-Territorial and Indigenous skills development and labour market programming. The federal government is also working with provinces and territories to increase Indigenous engagement with these fora to better respond to Indigenous labour market needs.

Understanding how employment programmes are implemented at the local level through case study analysis

This study analysed a number of local case studies to understand the implementation of the federal government's active labour market programming and its impact on Indigenous People. This report focuses on local activities in the following case study areas – all four of whom are agreement holders under ISET: Community Futures Treaty Seven (CFT7); the Centre for Aboriginal Human Resources and Development (CAHRD); Kiikenomaga Kikenjigewen Employment & Training Services (KKETS); and MAWIW Council.

Community Futures Treaty Seven

In the province of Alberta, Community Futures Treaty Seven (CFT7) supports all First Nation Individuals to obtain and maintain meaningful employment based on community needs through the provision of employment services in the Treaty Seven Territory. CFT7 provides employment related programmes and services in the following areas: General Labour Market; Youth Labour Market; Persons with Disabilities; and Child Care. CFT7 serves all Treaty Seven members or First Nations members with status at its 7 on-reserve employment centres and all urban Indigenous People who reside in the cities and surrounding area of one of its 4 urban centres located in Calgary, Red Deer, Lethbridge, and Medicine Hat.

Community Futures Treaty Seven also offers youth employment programmes (which fall under the federal government's Youth Programming) designed to ensure the economic prosperity of First Nations Treaty Status youth between the ages of 15-30. One such programme includes the First Nations Summer Career Placement Program which provides summer students with summer employment opportunities that try to develop skills that will stimulate valuable work experience for transitioning into the Alberta Labour Market. CFT7 targets placements that provide meaningful, career related work experience for post-secondary and secondary students with plans of returning to school upon completion of the summer placement.

The Centre for Aboriginal Human Resources Development (CAHRD)

In Winnipeg, Manitoba, the Centre for Aboriginal Human Resource Development (CAHRD) offers comprehensive services to Indigenous job-seekers that can lead directly to employment through job preparation (e.g. interview skills, résumé workshops, job referrals) or by creating a strategy for employment through further education and training (Shead, 2011).

CAHRD is a one-stop client service centre where a number of Indigenous non-governmental organisations (NGOs) now provide health, employment, literacy, education, training, and other support services to Winnipeg's Indigenous community. Their work and services focus on, and are coordinated to meet, the needs of Indigenous People as they adapt to the challenges of life in the more complex society of a modern urban setting.

CAHRD has three employment departments: Central Employment Services, Staffing Solutions and Aboriginal People with Disabilities Program. Employment Counsellors from each department meet with clients to discuss employment options, and help determine the best plan of action suitable to a person's needs, whether it be additional skills upgrading, or referral directly into a training programme (see Box 1.1).

Box 1.1. CAHRD's Central Employment Services

Central Employment Services help clients by creating an action plan to successfully attain career goals. Employment Counsellors offer career exploration options, referrals to employment, education and training, and job search strategies. This is achieved through:

- **One-on-one counselling services**: an Employment Counsellor will conduct an individual personal assessment to identify a client's marketable skills. They will assist in overcoming any barriers that may limit a client's employment opportunities and discuss an action plan for successfully attaining their personal career goals.
- **Referrals to academic upgrading or post-secondary training**: Employment Counsellors are available to discuss a client's options, and help determine the best plan of action suitable to their needs, including additional upgrading and referral directly into a training programme.
- **Free services**: CAHRD continues to offer step-by-step supports as clients identify, achieve and ultimately succeed with their goals.
- **Career exploration, training options, job search strategies and referrals, workshops and a computer resource centre** (computer lab, skills testing, faxing, printing, photocopying & voicemail) are available to clients free of charge.

The Central Employment Services, Staffing Solutions offers assistance to recent Indigenous graduates to find meaningful employment in their occupation of choice. Employment Counsellors will work one-on-one with clients to develop a customised plan and provide individual assistance to ensure their skills meet the demands of the workforce. In addition, they create partnerships with private and public sectors to establish employment opportunities for clients. Services include: One-on-one employment counselling; Short and long term goal setting; computer lab with internet access; connecting people with job leads and referrals; and job search workshops which cover résumé, cover letter, interview skills and mock interviews.

In addition, CAHRD also provides literacy through Neeginan Learning and Literacy and adult education through Aboriginal Community Campus for Indigenous adults. Technical and trades training is provided through its post-secondary training arm Neeginan Technical College (where programmes are developed and run based on the skill sets needed by the employer). All of CAHRD's services are coordinated around the needs of the Indigenous participants: from needing a referral to social services for survival money to being prepared to be successful in an interview for a job that pays CAD 26 per hour.

Kiikenomaga Kikenjigewen Employment & Training Services (KKETS)

In Thunder Bay, Ontario, Kiikenomaga Kikenjigewen Employment & Training Services (KKETS) is an agreement holder under ISET as well as the Skills and Partnerships Fund. Matawa First Nations is a Tribal Council providing services and programmes to eight Ojibway and Cree First Nations (Aroland, Constance Lake, Eabametoong, Ginoogaming, Marten Falls, Neskantaga, Nibinamik, and Webequie) in James Bay Treaty No. 9 and one First Nation (Long Lake #58) in the Robinson-Superior Treaty area. KKETS works with Employment Community Coordinators (ECC) in each First Nation community they represent to provide training programmes and to create employment opportunities for education, training and, employment for community members (KKETS, 2017).

Along with that, KKETS also works in partnerships with several organisations to deliver quality services and programmes to Matawa First Nations communities in Thunder Bay, including North Superior Workforce Planning Board (NSWPB), Confederation College, and Noront.

During the case study interviews, KKETS identifies remoteness, lack of programmes, funding and infrastructure, such as access to internet and roads, as the key economic development challenges facing their Indigenous communities. Many Matawa First Nations communities are small, rural, and some are even remote, which makes it difficult to have an ongoing and steady economy. Limited employment opportunities, and often, limited transportation to and from other communities, add additional barriers.

The Employment Integration Services Program (EISP) works with Matawa community members to remove barriers and obstacles to attaining employment. The programme helps participants by supplying a number of services, including resume writing, job search strategies, employment readiness assessments, work ethics training, and orientation sessions. In addition to assisting community members, the programme also provides cultural sensitivity awareness to employers through education and access to Elder supports, guiding and mentoring. Apart from those, KKETS also works externally with key organisations in delivering programmes and services that help build community capacity and increase community members' participation in the labour market workforce (KKETS, 2017).

As an example of a partnership with the Northern Policy Institute (NPI), NSWPB has developed the Baakaakonanen Ishkwandemonun (BI) - Opening Doors for You initiative, to acknowledge employers with inclusive hiring practices (see Box 1.2).

Box 1.2. Building local partnerships to find employment: Baakaakonanen Ishkwandemonun (BI)- Opening Doors for You initiative

Employers and service providers who assist job seekers in finding employment, get access to existing supports to hire from growing labour pools of newcomers and Indigenous People. As a result of the BI programme, Driving into the Future (DITF), emerged as a collaborative project between KKETS and NSWPB. In their regular interactions with KKETS staff Indigenous youth routinely identified not having a driver's license as a huge barrier to gaining employment outside of their communities, especially in large urban centres. This project funded 30 Indigenous youth from five fly-in or winter access road only communities to get their G1 licence. Out of the 30 students, 29 were successful in obtaining their G1 license. This programme sheds a light on this economic development issue many Matawa First Nation communities are facing, as youths from remote communities are unable to attain basic skills that are required to secure good employment.

MAWIW Council

MAWIW Council represents three First Nations' communities in New Brunswick: Esgenoôpetitj, Elsipogtog and Tobique First Nations. Through integrated partnerships, MAWIW works with organisations and government agencies to improve employment, economic development, health, and education service delivery.

Isolation, limited mobility, language and discrimination are major labour market challenges facing MAWIW First Nations' communities. All three MAWIW communities are situated in rural locations. From a geographic perspective, small isolated communities face additional barriers as they lack access to key resources typically found in an urban centre.

Even when community members have adequate employment skills, they face hardships in securing employment within or around their communities. The first issue is lack of employment opportunities available. However, given jobs are available in the nearest cities, members often hesitate to take them because it requires them moving away from their communities.

Those who wish to commute to work outside of the community also face challenges, as many communities are not serviced by public transit. Lack of driver's licences is an issue in rural communities as many cannot travel to the nearest office to take the test or they do not have access to training providers or vehicles to practice driving. To add, owning a vehicle is often out of reach for those who are in pre-employment stages. Thus, transportation creates a significant barrier for accessing training and employment opportunities.

Two additional central challenges are language and discrimination. New Brunswick is a bilingual province, which divides First Nations' people and creates linguistic enclaves. Bilingualism creates hurdles for MAWIW community members as it limits their employment opportunities, especially when securing full-time government jobs. Along with language barriers, Indigenous People also face discrimination when applying for jobs. Many organisations do not practice inclusive hiring practices; therefore many Indigenous People tend to face entrenched institutional racism in the labour market.

To overcome these challenges MAWIW works closely with their three communities in delivering several programmes such as the General Education development (GED) programme and the Aboriginal Skills and Employment Partnership (ASEP). Although ASEP expired in 2012, the success of the initiative contributed to the ISET programme which operates in every MAWIW community (see Box 1.3). The MAWIW ASEP project supported a broad scale partnership that allowed the MAWIW to work within their communities and build partnerships with industry in order to enable Indigenous People to access employment. This created a strong foundation for the partnerships that have been established within their communities to date.

Every MAWIW community also has an employment and training officer (ETO), who works with community members to develop employment goals and training plans. The ETO's then refer clients to the appropriate training provider or assist them in finding suitable employment. However economic development challenges limit job prospects in First Nations communities.

Box 1.3. Aboriginal Skills and Employment Partnership (ASEP) in Fredericton, New Brunswick

While it expired in 2012, the ASEP labour market initiative improved employment and training prospects for Indigenous People by supporting skills upgrading and providing on the job work experience opportunities that had lasting benefits for First Nations communities. The programme offered training in resource based sectors, such as forestry, mining, oil and gas, fishery, hydro development and construction (Aboriginal, 2008; Evaluation, 2015). Overall, 2 out of 5 ASEP participants (43%) were able to secure employment in the project's target industry. A large majority emphasized the importance of acquiring relevant education and skills, in attaining their employment (Summative, 2009). Thus, the ISET programme has built upon those results and used an integrated approach to help Indigenous workforce prepare for, find and maintain employment in the short and long-term.

Critical success factors identified from the case studies

There are a number of emerging success factors that have been identified from the in-depth fieldwork conducted as part of this OECD study, which can inform future policy and programme planning regarding the management and delivery of active labour market programmes.

Building the capacity of programmes managed and delivered by Indigenous People

The management and leadership of the Indigenous service delivery organisations analysed as part of this OECD study stressed the importance of having staff who are all Indigenous as a critical success factor in delivering employment programmes. Given the historical context in which Indigenous People have participated in government programmes, having front-line staff of Indigenous background ensures the appropriate cultural awareness of the barriers often faced by Indigenous People in looking for a job. This is critical in building trust with potential Indigenous job seekers, who often seek life-skills coaching and counselling as well as other pre-employment supports to ensure that they can remain in employment once they have successfully found a job.

Similar to views expressed during the federal government's consultations on the future of Indigenous labour market programming, there was common feedback among the case study areas on the need to strengthen the capacity of service delivery organisations. This means supporting the development of front-line employees, expanding employment counsellor training, and better supporting agreement holders in managing administrative requirements.

Leadership, governance, and partnerships

A key principle to guide the successful implementation of active labour market programmes across the case study areas is stable and strong leadership. The case study areas highlighted the importance of good governance within their organisation to guide the management and delivery of programmes. This means often having a dedicated board of governors led by Indigenous People that have a clear vision, mandate, and long-term view of the future.

Another clear success factor is working in partnership with other organisations within the community. It is important to establish a collaborative approach amongst communities, employers, local businesses, training providers and the provincial and federal government. More specifically, in order to increase labour force participation and align education and skills training with economic development initiatives, local Indigenous organisations need to be consistently engaged to discuss workforce gaps and arising opportunities. By having an open dialogue, local stakeholders can become aware of a communities' vision for the future and can better align programmes and services to meet Indigenous needs.

Programme flexibility

It is important to strike the right balance between accountability and flexibility. Currently, accountability provisions can be onerous both in terms of the frequency and length of reporting. A key guiding principle for federal programme design should be working with Indigenous communities versus administering a programme. Feedback from the case study areas stressed the importance of examining situations where increased programme flexibility can be designed to recognize local innovation and performance in addition to acknowledging the nation to nation relationship that is changing the functions of government relations between the federal government and Indigenous communities.

For example, federal active labour market programmes for Indigenous People have placed a strong emphasis on obtaining meaningful employment as a successful outcome of government intervention; however Indigenous People often face severe and multiple barriers to employment. Under the new ISET program currently being co-implemented with Indigenous partners, more emphasis will be placed on overall outcome progression along the skills development continuum. This will allow agreement holders to deliver services to clients facing multiple barriers who might require more pre-employment supports.

Feedback from the case study areas suggests that there are potential benefits of putting in place longer term funding agreements for service delivery. The new ISETs program is addressing this issue extending current arrangements from five to 10 years. This is consistent with feedback through the federal government's engagement process with Indigenous communities where there was a consensus on the need to extend the length of active labour market programmes to allow agreement holders to undertake longer-term planning, to support Indigenous People for longer interventions, and identify results over a longer timeframe.

Developing robust local labour market information

To correctly tailor employment and training programmes it is important to carefully analyse the current and estimated labour market supply and demand factors in the local labour market. Across the case study areas, a barrier that First Nations' community developers and leaders face is an insufficient/inadequate knowledge of the current labour skills and the business capacity of their people. Not having a solid understanding of workforce needs prevents Indigenous communities from developing appropriate programmes and services to advance community employment and economic growth.

Secondly, if leaders are not fully aware of the rising needs or opportunities in their communities, they cannot adequately advocate or negotiate terms for building community capacity with other key organisations. In New Brunswick, Esgenoôpetitj and Elsipogtog First Nations overcame that barrier by partnering up with JEDI to create a workforce database which helps connect community members with employment opportunities. For example, Working Warriors is an online tool which community members can use to create or upload their resumes and apply for jobs within New Brunswick. This tool helps communities capture their workforce's skills capacity and then utilize that information to assist members with job readiness and employability skills (Working Warriors in New Brunswick, 2015; Joint Economic Development of First Nations Communities: Institutional Arrangements, 2016). Community leaders can now work together with external organisations to create a comprehensive strategic workforce development plan.

Notes

1. Statistics Canada states that "The participation rate is the number of labour force participants expressed as a percentage of the population 15 years of age and over. The participation rate for a particular group (age, sex, marital status, etc.) is the number of labour force participants in that group expressed as a percentage of the population for that group. Estimates are percentages, rounded to the nearest tenth" (Statistics Canada, 2016e).
2. Statistics Canada states that "The employment rate is the number of persons employed expressed as a percentage of the population 15 years of age and over. The employment rate for a particular group (age, sex, marital status, etc.) is the number employed in that group expressed as a percentage of the population for that group. Estimates are percentages, rounded to the nearest tenth" (Statistics Canada, 2016e).
3. The data that is available and being analysed for this section is from the Labour Force Survey and excludes on-reserve, the Northwest Territories, the Yukon and Nunavut. It is important to note that the inequality demonstrated would likely be more significant if the data included on-reserve and territorial population labour market indicators.
4. Formerly known as the Aboriginal Skills and Employment Training Strategy (ASETS).

References

Aboriginal Affairs and Northern Development Canada (2013), Aboriginal Demographics From the 2011 National Household Survey, https://www.aadnc-aandc.gc.ca/DAM/DAM-INTER-HQ-AI/STAGING/texte-text/abo_demo2013_1370443844970_eng.pdf (accessed on 23 June 2017).

Arriagada, P. (2016), Women in Canada: A Gender-based Statistical Report, Minister of Industry, http://www.statcan.gc.ca/pub/89-503-x/2015001/article/14313-eng.htm (accessed on 23 June 2017).

Economic Development of First Nations Communities: Institutional Arrangements (2003). Auditor General of Canada. Retrieved from http://www.oag-bvg.gc.ca/internet/docs/20031109ce.pdf.

Employment and Social Development Canada (2017), Aboriginal skills and employment training strategy (ASETS) terms and conditions for contributions - Canada.ca, https://www.canada.ca/en/employment-social-development/services/indigenous/asets-terms-conditions.html (accessed on 6 November 2017).

Indigenous and Northern Affairs Canada (2013), Aboriginal Demographics from the 2011 National Household Survey, https://www.aadnc-aandc.gc.ca/eng/1370438978311/1370439050610 (accessed on 30 October 2017).

KKETS (2017), Employment & Training Services, http://www.kkets.ca/ (accessed on 13 February 2018).

OECD (2016), Employment and Skills Strategies in Saskatchewan and the Yukon, Canada, OECD Reviews on Local Job Creation, OECD Publishing, Paris, http://dx.doi.org/10.1787/9789264259225-en.

OECD (2017), Unemployment rate (indicator), https://data.oecd.org/unemp/unemployment-rate.htm (accessed on 23 June 2017), http://dx.doi.org/10.1787/997c8750-en.

OECD (2017), Employment Outlook 2017: How does Canada Compare?, https://www.oecd.org/canada/Employment-Outlook-CANADA-EN.pdf (accessed on 23 June 2017), http://dx.doi.org/10.1787/empl_outlook-2017-en.

Shead, W. (2011), Cora J. Voyageur (ed.), Dream and Today's Reality: Aboriginal Centre of Winnipeg - Adapting to Urban Life in Canada, University of Toronto Press.

Sinclair, M. (2010), For the child take, for the parent left behind, United Nations Permanent Forum on Indigenous Issues, http://www.trc.ca/websites/trcinstitution/File/pdfs/TRC_UN_Speech_CMS_FINAL_April_27_2010.pdf (accessed on 30 October 2017).

Statistics Canada (2011a). Aboriginal Peoples: Fact Sheet for Canada. [Online]
Available at: http://www.statcan.gc.ca/pub/89-656-x/89-656-x2015001-eng.htm#n5 (accessed 27 June 2017).

Statistics Canada (2011b), Public Use Microdata Files (PUMFs), National Household Survey (NHS), 2011, Author's calculations, http://www12.statcan.gc.ca/nhs-enm/2011/dp-pd/pumf-fmgd/index-eng.cfm (accessed on 30 October 2017).

Statistics Canada (2011c), Table 4: Age distribution and median age for selected Aboriginal identity categories, http://www12.statcan.gc.ca/nhs-enm/2011/as-sa/99-011-x/2011001/tbl/tbl04-eng.cfm (accessed on 23 June 2017).

Statistics Canada (2015), Aboriginal Statistics at a Glance: 2nd Edition, http://www.statcan.gc.ca/pub/89-645-x/89-645-x2015001-eng.pdf (accessed on 10 July 2017).

Statistics Canada (2016a), Aboriginal Peoples in Canada: First Nations People, Métis and Inuit, http://www12.statcan.gc.ca/nhs-enm/2011/as-sa/99-011-x/99-011-x2011001-eng.cfm (accessed on 15 June 2017).

Statistics Canada (2016b), 2016 Census, Catalogue Number 98-400-X2016357.

Statistics Canada (2016c), 2016 Census, Catalogue Number 98-400-X2016359.

Statistics Canada (2016d), 2016 Census, Catalogue Number 98-400-X2016265.

Statistics Canada (2016e), 2016 Census, Catalogue Number 98-400-X2016174.

Statistics Canada (2016f), Census of Population. Canada and census metropolitan areas and census agglomerations, 2016 Census – 25% Sample data, data extracted by Employment and Skills Development Canada, received 11 April 2018.

Statistics Canada (2016g), Labour force, employment and unemployment, levels and rates, by province, http://www.statcan.gc.ca/tables-tableaux/sum-som/l01/cst01/labor07a-eng.htm (accessed on 23 June 2017).

Statistics Canada (2016h), Table 282-0002 - Labour Force Survey estimates (LFS), by sex and detailed age group, annual (persons unless otherwise noted), CANSIM (database) (accessed on 2 May 2018)

Statistics Canada (2017a), Aboriginal Peoples Highlight Tables, 2016 Census, 2016 NHS, http://www12.statcan.gc.ca/census-recensement/2016/dp-pd/hlt-fst/abo-aut/Table.cfm?Lang=Eng&T=102&S=88&O=A (accessed on 30 October 2017).

Statistics Canada (2017b), Aboriginal identity population by age and sex, Catalogue no.:
98-402-X2016009, National Household Survey 2016, available at http://www12.statcan.gc.ca/census-recensement/2016/dp-pd/hlt-fst/abo-aut/index-eng.cfm.

Statistics Canada (2017c), Aboriginal identity population by both sexes, total - age, 2016 counts, Canada, provinces and territories, 2016 Census – 25% Sample data, Aboriginal Peoples Highlight Tables, 2016 Census, http://www12.statcan.gc.ca/census-recensement/2016/dp-pd/hlt-fst/abo-aut/Table.cfm?Lang=Eng&T=101&D1=1&D2=1&D3=1&RPP=25&PR=0&SR=1&S=102&O=D (accessed on 25 January 2018).

Statistics Canada (2017d), The Aboriginal population in Canada, 2016 Census of Population, NHS 2016, http://www.statcan.gc.ca/pub/11-627-m/11-627-m2017027-eng.htm (accessed on 30 October 2017).

Statistics Canada (2017e), Aboriginal peoples in Canada: Key results from the 2016 Census, The Daily, http://www.statcan.gc.ca/daily-quotidien/171025/dq171025a-eng.htm (accessed on 10 December 2017).

Statistics Canada (2017f). Multifactor and labour productivity in the aggregate business sector and major sub-sectors, by North American Industry Classification System (NAICS).

Statistics Canada (2017k), Table 251-0022 - Adult correctional services, custodial admissions to provincial and territorial programs by Aboriginal identity, annual (number), CANSIM (database) (accessed on 3 July 2017).

Statistics Canada (2017j), Table 282-0226- Labour force survey estimates (LFS), by Aboriginal group, sex and age group, Canada, selected provinces and regions, annual (persons), CANSIM (database), (accessed on 3 July 2017).

Statistics Canada (2017l), Table 282-0233 - Labour force survey estimates (LFS), average hourly and weekly wages and average usual weekly hours by Aboriginal group and age group, Canada, selected provinces and regions, 2007-2016.

Truth and Reconciliation Commission of Canada (2015), Truth and Reconciliation Commission of Canada: Calls to Action, Truth and Reconciliation Commission of Canada, Winnipeg, http://www.trc.ca/websites/trcinstitution/File/2015/Findings/Calls_to_Action_English2.pdf (accessed on 30 October 2017).

Working Warriors in New Brunswick (2015),
Retrieved from http://www.workingwarriors.ca/Projects/newbrunswick.

Chapter 2. Improving local skills training for Indigenous People in Canada

In Canada, the overall educational attainment of Indigenous People falls behind the non-Indigenous population. Skills are a key route out of poverty and provide a solid foundation for Indigenous People to participate in the labour market. This chapter looks at key barriers to educational attainment of Indigenous Canadians as well as recent skills programmes that have been implemented at the federal and local level.

Understanding the skills outcomes of Indigenous People

In the TRC's Calls to Action, education was identified as a key issue and significant barrier to the labour market success of Indigenous People. The TRC pointed out the need to provide equal education funding for Indigenous children; protect Indigenous languages, culture and history by integrating these important topics in curriculum; including Indigenous parents and community in decisions regarding their children's education, honouring Treaty relationships and developing more Early Childhood Education and Care (ECEC) programmes for Indigenous children (Truth and Reconciliation Commission of Canada, 2015).

Blair Stonechild (2006), a professor and Cree-Saulteaux member of the Muscowpetung First Nation, explains that elders referred to education as 'new buffalo. In an interview with the University of Regina (June, 2010), he elaborates:

"When you look at traditional culture, the buffalo probably provided 95% of all the things that they needed. With the buffalo gone, the question became what replaces it? When you take a look at the struggle in the treaties, the way they were negotiated and the foresight of the negotiators, education was the thing that would guarantee the ability of First Nations people to survive in this new world. So that is basically the concept, that the new buffalo is access to education – not just elementary and secondary, but post-secondary as well" (Stonechild, 2016).

Building the educational and skills levels of the Indigenous population will require concerted efforts to mentor Indigenous youth about the value of participating in the education system and to support educational institutes in providing and maintaining quality and culturally sensitive education to Indigenous students, from primary to post-secondary levels. Such supports should focus on ensuring student retention and nurturing Indigenous student in their development in socially and psychologically safe settings.

Education and skills outcomes

The OECD report, *Promising Practices in Supporting Success for Indigenous Students* documents differences in participation rates, attendance rates, expulsion rates and graduation rates between Indigenous and non-Indigenous students in Canada; Queensland, Australia; and New Zealand. The report found that enrolment rates for four year-olds Indigenous students were less than 20% in Alberta, Manitoba, Nova Scotia and the Yukon in 2015. In the same year, the largest gaps between Indigenous and non-Indigenous enrolment in Canada were at the ages five and six year-olds, with still less than 80% of Indigenous children enrolled in school. Otherwise, comparing Indigenous enrolment in Alberta, Manitoba, Nova Scotia and Yukon between 2010 and 2015, the enrolment rates were consistent around 80% with marginal improvements for five, six and seven year-olds (OECD, 2017a).

In regards to differences in the number of days absent per year in 2015, a consistent gap of at least ten days was reported between Indigenous and non-Indigenous students from the ages 13-18 within Nova Scotia and Yukon. However, in regards the number of days absent for male and female Indigenous students, there appeared to be very little difference in their outcomes in the year 2015. In 2015, the number of days Indigenous students are absent in Queensland and New Zealand is about ten days or less at each age (from age eight) compared to Indigenous students in Nova Scotia and Yukon (OECD, 2017a).

Promising Practices in Supporting Success for Indigenous Students did report an improvement in Indigenous graduation rates for the Canadian provinces of Alberta and Manitoba between 2010 (about 40%) and 2015 (about 53%) of more than 10%. However, Alberta and Manitoba's performances still were about 15% less than the graduation rates of Indigenous students in Queensland and New Zealand. Differences in graduation rates were most striking between Indigenous and non-Indigenous groups which graduated Indigenous males (52%) and females (54%) at least 30% less than non-Indigenous males (82%) and females (87%) (OECD, 2017a).

While 60% of Indigenous People did not have a post-secondary certificate according to the 2016 Census, the Indigenous post-secondary certificate holders primarily studied trades, services, natural resources and conservation (14.4%); business and administration (6.5%) and health care (5.8%)(Statistics Canada, 2016a).

In comparison, about 44% of non-Indigenous People did not obtain post-secondary certificates. Of the ones who did acquire the certification, the non-Indigenous students were represented more than twice Indigenous students within arts and humanities (5.1%); engineering and engineering technology (4.9%); science and science technology (3%); and mathematics, computer and information science (2.3%) (Statistics Canada, 2016a). Furthermore, Figure 5.2 contrasts employment rates of Indigenous People with those of non-Indigenous People by major field of study. This figure demonstrates that in addition to an underrepresentation in major fields of study that lead to work in knowledge sectors, Indigenous People more often than not have lower employment rates in these majors. Differences in employment rates between Indigenous and Non-Indigenous graduates can be seen in majors such as agriculture, natural resources and conservation (8% gap); mathematics, computer and information sciences (6.1% gap); and architecture, engineering, and related technologies (4.8% gap). Only within the major of education are the employment rate outcomes most strikingly inversed with Indigenous People having an 11% higher employment rate than non-Indigenous People (Statistics Canada, 2016b).

Figure 2.1. Highest level of education attained, Indigenous status, %, 2016

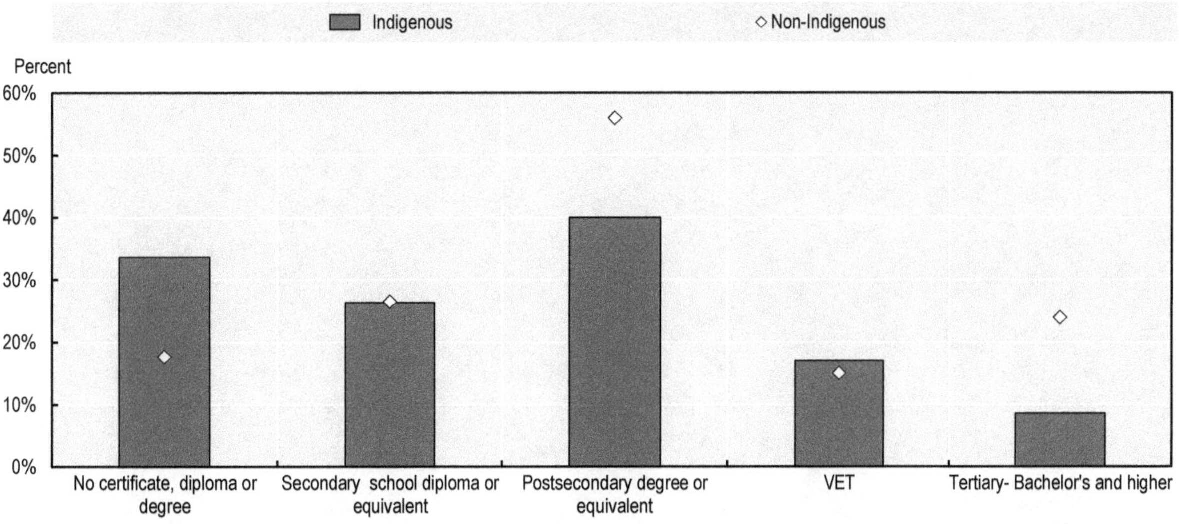

Source: Statistics Canada (2016), 2016 Census, Statistics Canada, Catalogue no. 98-400-X2016262.

StatLink http://dx.doi.org/10.1787/888933724024

Figure 2.2. Employment rate by major field of study, Indigenous status, %, ages 15 years or older, 2016

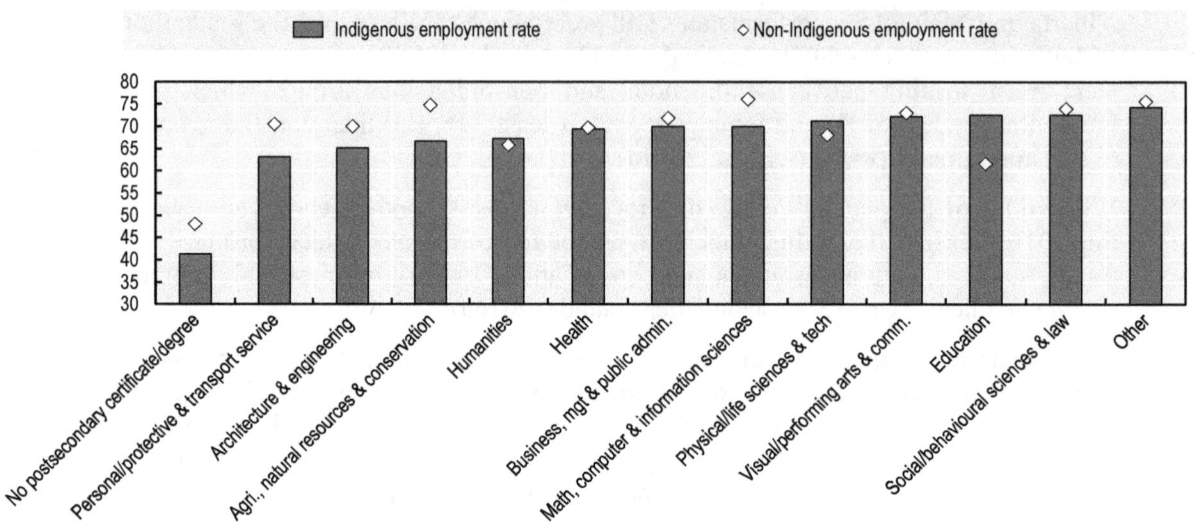

Note: Excludes census data for one or more incompletely enumerated Indian reserves or Indian settlements.
Source : Statistics Canada (2016), 2016 Census, Catalogue no. 98-400-X2016267.

StatLink http://dx.doi.org/10.1787/888933724043

At the level of cities, differences in tertiary educational attainment are quite visible as well. Percentage gaps between Indigenous and non-Indigenous groups are the largest in Vancouver (18.9%) and Calgary (18.4%). However, Québec City has the lowest gap in outcomes with a difference of 7.7% (Statistics Canada, 2016c). Comparing Vocational Education and Training (VET), the outcome gaps between Indigenous and non-Indigenous groups are far lower. In Thunder Bay, outcomes between the two groups are inversed. However, this might be explained due to industries in the region relying more on skills acquired through VET programmes (Statistics Canada, 2016c).

Figure 2.3. Percentage of Indigenous and non-Indigenous adults (15 years and older) having completed tertiary education (Bachelor's and above), most-populated Canadian metropolitan areas, 2016

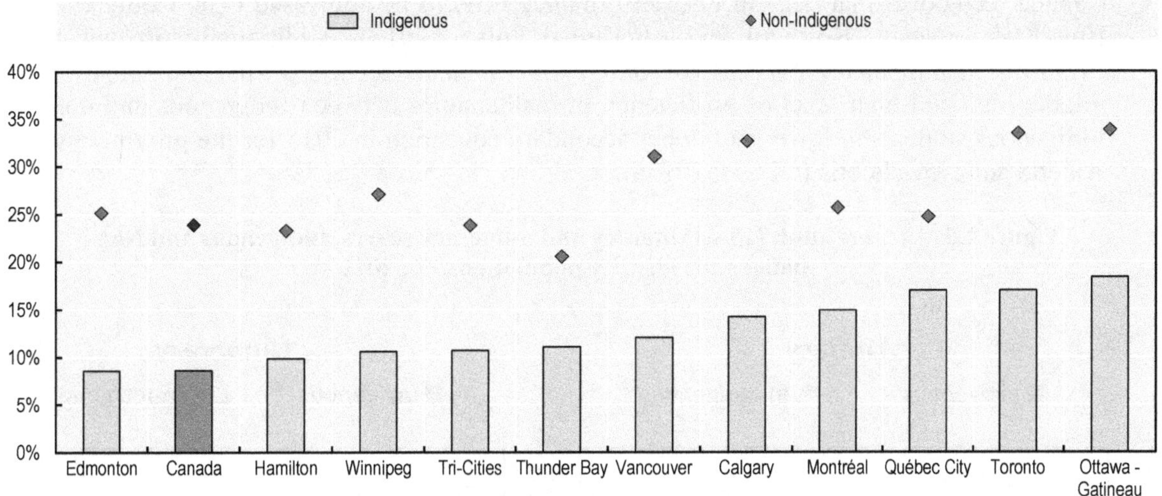

Note: Thunder Bay refers to the Census Metropolitan Area (CMA) of Greater Sudbury – Thunder Bay. Tri-Cities stands for Kitchener-Cambridge-Waterloo CMA.

Source: Statistics Canada (2016), 2016 Census of Population. Canada and census metropolitan areas and census agglomerations, 2016 Census – 25% Sample data, data extracted by Employment and Skills Development Canada, received 11 April 2018.

StatLink http://dx.doi.org/10.1787/888933724062

Figure 2.4. Percentage of Indigenous and non-Indigenous adults (15 years and older) who participated in VET, most-populated Canadian metropolitan areas, 2016

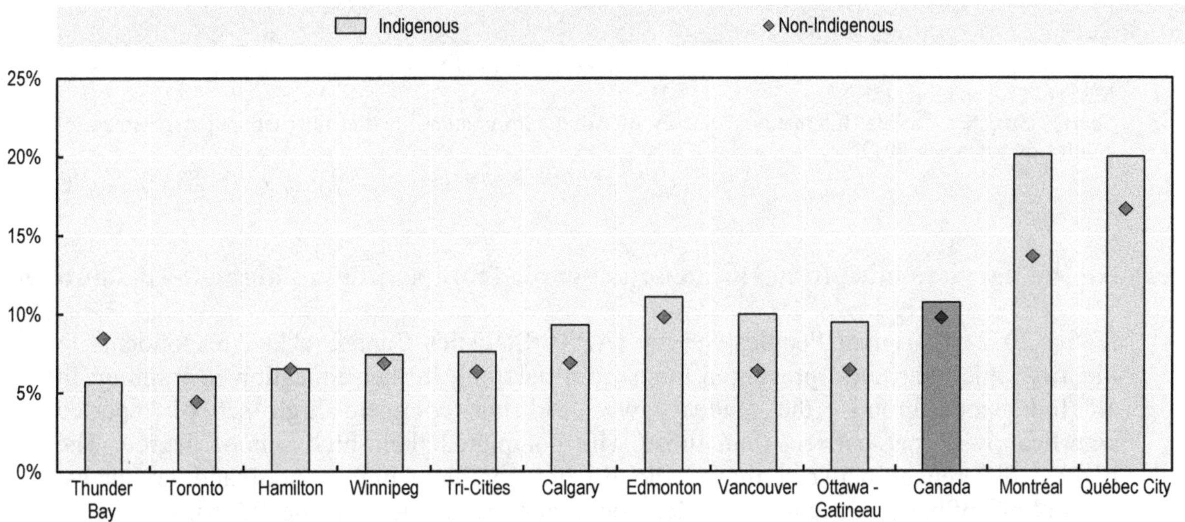

Note: Thunder Bay refers to the Census Metropolitan Area (CMA) of Greater Sudbury – Thunder Bay. Tri-Cities stands for Kitchener-Cambridge-Waterloo CMA.

Source: Statistics Canada, 2016 Census of Population. Canada and census metropolitan areas and census agglomerations, 2016 Census – 25% Sample data, data extracted by Employment and Skills Development Canada, received 11 April 2018.

StatLink http://dx.doi.org/10.1787/888933724081

Educational performance

In their analysis of Indigenous People's test scores for the Programme for the International Assessment of Adult Competencies (PIAAC), the Conference Board of Canada recognises that gaps in test performance need to be addressed (The Conference Board of Canada - Northern and Aboriginal Policy, 2017). Additionally, *Promising Practices in Supporting Success for Indigenous Students* reports a 20% gap in lower middle-high and high level of proficiency in mathematics between Indigenous and non-Indigenous students in lower and upper secondary education in 2015 for the provinces of Alberta and Nova Scotia (OECD, 2017a).

Figure 2.5. Average adult (15-64) literacy and numeracy scores, Indigenous and Non-Indigenous identity populations, %, 2012

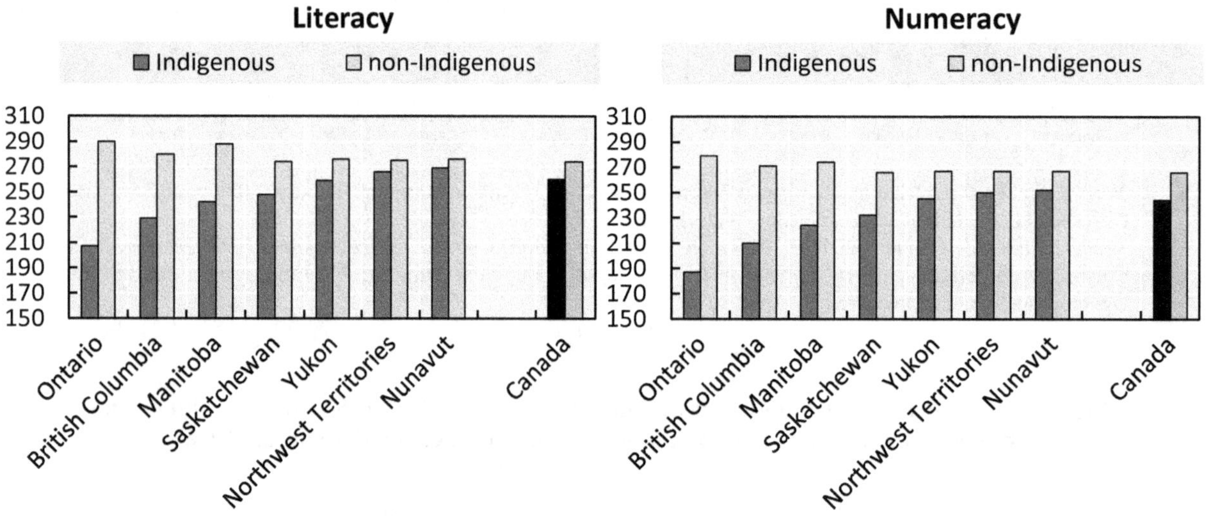

Note: Indigenous Peoples surveyed in PIAAC are composed of First Nations people living off reserve (48%), Métis (44%), and Inuit (5%).

Source: Statistics Canada, International Survey of Adults, Programme for the International Assessment of Adult Competencies, 2012.

StatLink http://dx.doi.org/10.1787/888933724100

What are the barriers inhibiting Indigenous People from acquiring higher skills outcomes?

In the 2012 Aboriginal Peoples Survey (APS), Statistics Canada asked respondents to identify which barrier(s) prevented them from pursuing further education or training. In all Indigenous groups, the students who did not complete high school reported significantly higher barriers than those who completed their high school degree. The highest differences between those who do not complete high school and graduates' perceptions of barriers occur in the Métis population (Statistics Canada, 2015).

For leavers within each Indigenous group, the barriers with the highest percent of responses were courses not matching needs, the cost, personal and family responsibilities and a lack of personal priority. While each category needs to be addressed, the highest barriers for those who did not complete high school should be prioritized (Statistics Canada, 2015).

Access to Early Childhood Education and Care

The OECD's *Starting Strong 2017: Key OECD Indicators on Early Childhood Education and Care* articulates how children's participation in ECEC can heavily impact the lives of individuals through their life. *Starting Strong 2017* cites data from the Programme for International Student Assessment (PISA). PISA test results indicate that ECEC is the strongest predictor for high (or low) PISA test results than any other indicator. Moreover, the OECD specifies that at least two years of participation in ECEC are needed for the experience to have an impact on 15-year-olds PISA test performance (OECD, 2017d).

In Canada, *Promising Practices in Supporting Success for Indigenous Students* reports that less than 90% of Indigenous students participate in ECEC (however, this number is an estimate due to differences in Indigenous self-identification processes within the census and within schools).

Housing conditions

The conditions children live in at home greatly influence their performance at school. Inadequate and substandard housing conditions can have a negative impact on their performance and wellbeing. In regards to housing, Statistics Canada reports that 18.3% of Indigenous People were living in crowded dwellings in 2016 (Statistics Canada, 2017). In contrast, only 8.5% of non-Indigenous People live in crowded dwellings during the same period (Statistics Canada, 2017). In addition, 19.4% of Indigenous People's homes require major repairs (Statistics Canada, 2017).

Language

The Conference Board of Canada highlights that when viewing the test results and overall performances of Indigenous students in educational systems, one should consider that 15% of Indigenous People reported an Indigenous language as their mother tongue in the 2011 NHS (The Conference Board of Canada - Northern and Aboriginal Policy, 2017). The 2016 Census showed similar results, with 15.6% of Indigenous People speaking an Indigenous language (Statistics Canada, 2017).

Therefore, while the scores do reflect the need to further improve attainment and quality of education for Indigenous People, the French and English versions of the PIAAC test may not be the best testing mechanism for students who do not have those languages as their native language. Furthermore, Indigenous students can also encounter language barriers regarding the language of instruction at schools and educational materials such as textbooks.

Learning difficulties

Data from Nova Scotia and Yukon within *Promising Practices in Supporting Success for Indigenous Students* indicates that there are far more Indigenous students assessed with learning difficulties in those regions. 15% of Indigenous children at age nine are accessed with learning difficulties compared to less than 10% of non-Indigenous students. The number of Indigenous students accessed with learning difficulties climaxes at age 14, at just less than 25% of students. In comparison, just above 10% of non-Indigenous children are assessed with learning difficulties at the same age (OECD, 2017a). More policy research needs to be undertaken to understand these critical issues in order to develop policies and strategies to resolve them.

What policies and programmes have been implemented to address the skills outcomes of Indigenous People in Canada?

The United Nations Declaration on the Rights of Indigenous Peoples (UNDRIP) underlines the right for Indigenous families and communities to be active participants in their children's education. In particular, Articles 14 and 21 explicitly define the educational rights of Indigenous People. These articles specify Indigenous People's rights to further their own languages, cultures, traditions and knowledge through the management of their own educational systems and institutions. They also have the right to the improvement of these institutions and the right to participate in these institutions without discrimination (United Nations, 2008).

In May 2016, Canada became a full supporter of UNDRIP. While gaps in educational and skills attainment persist for Indigenous People, several policies and programmes have been introduced or are in place to build the skills of Indigenous People work towards the actualisation of rights for Indigenous People.

Skills and Partnership Fund

The Skills and Partnership Fund (SPF) is a proposal-based programme that encourages stakeholders, such as training institutions, community organisations, local business and industry, to partner with Indigenous organisations to support skills development, job training and employment supports for Indigenous People. These partnerships are intended to address a broad range of Indigenous socio-economic issues, while also better meeting local labour market demand.

SPF was launched in 2010, with an investment of 210 million CAD over five years to support service delivery; skills development, including essential skills training; and training-to-employment for jobs identified by partner employers. In 2015, the federal government announced the renewal of the Skills and Partnership Fund's (SPF) with annual funding of CAD 50 million until March 31, 2021. The fourth and most recent Call for Proposals was launched on 24 May 2016 and closed on 29 July 2016 with 230 proposals received and a total funding request of CAD 935.5 million. The call sought proposals from all sectors and focused on improving employment outcomes under two funding streams:

- Training-to-Employment: encourage an increased number of employed clients in skilled, long-term jobs and the level of partnership funding, and
- Innovation: enhance the employability of Indigenous People by addressing a broader range of socio-economic challenges within Indigenous communities.

SPF is inherently partnership-based and requires the continuous engagement of Indigenous partners, with the involvement of provincial/territorial governments and private sector stakeholders where relevant. The SPF is demand-driven and supports government priorities through strategic partnerships by funding projects contributing to the skills development and training of Indigenous workers for long-term, meaningful employment in high-skilled and in-demand fields.

The SPF encourages Indigenous organisations to form partnerships with governments, businesses, and community organisations to improve skills training and create jobs and opportunities for Indigenous People. Strategic partnerships are a mandatory element of this application-based programme with SPF projects leveraging ESDC funding with partner contributions. Designed to complement the ISET programme, the SPF programme promotes innovation and co-operation, tests new approaches to the delivery of employment services, and addresses gaps in service delivery to improve employment outcomes for Indigenous People. The programme fosters more integrated, harmonized training-to-employment models and acts as a catalyst for the forming and testing of innovative new partnerships in Indigenous labour market development. This leads to improved programme effectiveness, efficiency, and overall reach of the ISET network.

Since 2012, over 30 000 Indigenous People have participated in the SPF programme, of which over 12 700 individuals have become employed and over 1 600 have returned to school. The SPF programme has also leveraged approximately CAD 250 million from 2010 to 2017 in financial and in-kind support from over 400 partners in the private sector and other organizations.

Income assistance for youth

The Government of Canada provides case management services for youth, ages 18 to 24 years old, living on-reserve and in the Yukon who are recipients of Income Assistance. The purpose of these Income Assistance Pre-employment Supports is to improve basic life skills, including numeracy and literacy, with the view of improving access to education and employment specific training. Canada's 2017 Federal Budget provided CAD 39 million to these activities in 2017-2018. The Income Assistance Pre-employment Supports are implemented in collaboration with 22 service providers, bands and tribal councils that serve a total of 110 First Nations communities.

Apprenticeship programmes

Apprenticeships have been identified as an effective mechanism for smoothing the transition for young people between school and the world of work. While apprenticeships and work-based learning opportunities have demonstrable benefits for young people and employers, many countries face a number of barriers to broadening their availability. Apprenticeship programmes, which combine workplace learning with classroom instruction, have been demonstrated to be a useful training arrangement, which are well linked to labour market opportunities (OECD, 2017b). There are many programmes across Canada designed to introduce Indigenous People to apprenticeship opportunities. Looking at educational outcomes (previous Figure 5.1), Indigenous People are already over-represented within vocational education and training relative to the non-Indigenous People.

A previous OECD report (*OECD Reviews on Local Job Creation: Employment and Skills Strategies in Canada*) provides an overview of Canada's apprenticeship system. (OECD, 2014) In sum, the Canadian Apprenticeship Forum (CAF) notes the training combines alternating periods of on-the-job (80-90%) and technical training (10-20%). After completing both the classroom and the on-the-job training, apprentices can receive a Certificate of Apprenticeship (for non-restricted trades) or a Certificate of Qualification (for restricted trades). Depending on the trade, it takes about two to five years as an apprentice to become a certified journeyperson. Each province and territory has its own training and certification policies and its own list of designated apprenticeship programmes.

The federal government supports apprenticeship certifications through a Red Seal Programme, which promotes a set of common standards that allow the recognition of certifications across provincial jurisdictions. While professional certificates or licenses are recognised by all provincial jurisdictions under the Agreement on Internal Trade

(AIT), the Red Seal provides the assurance that workers are qualified according to common standards of knowledge and competency as defined by industry.

Furthermore, as part of the federal government's Budget 2018, the federal government announced the Pre-Apprenticeship Program which will provide $46 million over five years, starting with $6 million in 2018–19, and $10 million per year thereafter, for the Program. The new programme will focus on supporting those that are underrepresented and disadvantaged in the trades, such as women, youth, Indigenous Peoples, newcomers and people with disabilities

The Canadian Council of Directors of Apprenticeship (CCDA) is responsible for the management of the Red Seal Programme. The CCDA works with industry to facilitate the development of a skilled labour force, and labour mobility across Canada. One of the best solutions to support the interests of both employers and prospective Indigenous employees has been through the use of apprenticeship programmes. As apprentices gain new skills through applied learning, employers use the experience to invest organisational knowledge in apprentices and determine if they are a good fit for further employment.

Previous OECD work has highlighted examples of Indigenous Communities investing in apprenticeship training. For example, the Tr'ondëk Hwëch'in in the Yukon acts as an intermediary between employers and the vocational education system, minimising the administrative burden for employers. Both the apprenticeship programme and the intermediary role of the Tr'ondëk Hwëch'in First Nation give employers the incentive to take hiring risks that they would not otherwise (OECD, 2017c).

Understanding how training and skills development programmes are being implemented through case study analysis

Centre for Aboriginal Human Resources and Development (CAHRD)

CAHRD provides a holistic approach to education through individualised support services, including access to employment, academic and personal counselling. They offer student housing, on-site subsidised day care, and health and wellness activities. CAHRD provides quality education and training programmes through partnerships with the local community, education institutions, business, industry, and government (Shead, 2011). CAHRD has initiated five programmes that have their own institutional identities but operate as programmes of CAHRD. These include the following:

- An **Aboriginal Community Campus**, which provides educational upgrading in math, English, chemistry, physics, biology, political science, and native languages;
- **Neeginan College of Applied Technology**, which provides training in technical courses such as early childhood education, carpentry, and accounting, and positions such as building systems technician, medical laboratory technician, licensed practical nurse, educational assistant, and glassworker technician;
- **Kookum's Place Daycare**, a non-profit agency, which is licensed for forty-nine children of ages three months to six years;
- **Neeginan Village**, a forty-two-unit students' housing complex, and
- **Aboriginal Aerospace Initiative**, an innovative programme for training up to two hundred Indigenous People for skilled jobs in the aerospace industry.

Synergies between these programmes provide Indigenous learners with a seamless transition from literacy and upgrading, through post-secondary training and to sustainable employment. New applicants to any Education or Training programme must attend a CAHRD Orientation Session and complete a Level Placement Test (LPT).

CAHRD offers literacy, education, post-secondary training to Indigenous People in Winnipeg. Neeginan College of Applied Technology, CAHRD's post-secondary training division offers post-secondary programming mainly in industrial trades. Recently, Neeginan College was awarded funding through Western Economic Diversification Canada for its Computer Numerical Control (CNC) programme. The funding will be used to purchase state-of-the-art equipment so that programme trainees are trained on the most efficient and most technological advanced machinery available.

CNC Operators oversee the operation of all CNC equipment, often operating three or four machines at a time in larger manufacturing facility. Most operators are employed in the fabricated metal, machinery and plastics products manufacturing industries and require skills to operate or run the CNC Machine – not how to design one.

CAHRD's CNC Machine Program is designed to be 8 months in length and to accommodate 12 to 16 students in each offering. The programme is offered on a continuous repeating cycle basis (every 8 to 9 months). The curriculum consists of Math, Blue Print Reading, Safety and Precision Measurement, Technical training including 25% theory and 75% practical, and concluding with a one-month work practicum.

Applicants who require pre-programme training will be enrolled in Pre- Trades Preparation, which would consist of trades specific upgrading, Essential Skills, high school Math and English, and employability skills. The length of this pre-programme would be specific to the individual applicant's needs, ranging from one month to three or four months.

In general, skills development programming has increasingly become more employer/industry driven. Neeginan College has developed industry advisory committees for all of its training programmes, which facilitates on-going industry input into programme development and delivery.

Community Futures Treaty Seven (CFT7)

One of the more successful programmes for skills training that was cited by CFT7 (and in which they were a key implementing partner) is Trade Winds to Success. This programme is designed as a recruitment and pre-apprenticeship programme to assist Indigenous People into Alberta companies. Typical jobs that are the target of training included carpenter, electrician, iron worker, steam fitter, insulator, and millwright. The goal of the programme was to address the estimated shortfall of Skilled Trades People in Alberta over next decade.

The programme begins with a three week trade streaming process involving: assessment testing and visits to training sites, shops and local education facilities. Participants then go to an Informed Career Decision Making course to ensure they choose to study the trade that is right for them. After this, they move to the pre-apprenticeship training which includes: personal development (one week); academic upgrading (four weeks); writing an Entrance Exam 4 from Apprenticeship Industry and Trades; progress to eight weeks of union shop and hand tools training; employment a unions or employer of choice; and mentorship.

One of the key features of the programme is following up with individuals 6, and 12 months after their participation. It was an Indigenous staffed programme for Indigenous learners, which created a sense of belonging and trust among participants. Since 2005, there have been 52 programme intakes, with around 800 students graduated and 710 students finding a job (e.g. 90% placement rate). Trade Winds to Success is designed as a partnership between government, industry, Indigenous communities and unions. Unique supports were offered to students and mentorship was delivered at each stage of programme delivery by dedicated staff.

Trade Winds to Success Training Society is an Indigenous organisation that is supported through the Skills and Partnerships Fund (SPF) from July 2017 to March 2021 with a contribution from Employment and Social Development Canada of CAD 7.99 million. This organisation was previously support by ESDC through the SPF from February 2013 to March 2017. CFT7 contributed as a key project partner.

Kiikenomaga Kikenjigewen Employment & Training Services (KKETS)

Prominent labour market and skills development challenges facing Matawa First Nations communities include: remoteness of communities, shortage of jobs, and lack of education and experience to fill available employment opportunities. There is also a gap between the skills needed in the job market versus the skills the community members possess. This mismatch in skills poses a big labour market challenge for Matawa First Nations communities. With that, barriers such as mobility and education create additional obstacles for members to acquire well-paying employment.

To counter labour market and skills development challenges, KKETS offers several programmes, which provide skills upgrading opportunities to Matawa community members. The Aboriginal Skills Development Program (ASAP), allows adult learners to earn their Ontario Secondary School Diploma (OSSD), giving them the opportunity to pursue further post-secondary education and skilled trades training offered by KKETS. Employment readiness training is built into the programme to provide individuals with life skills training and basic employment certifications such as First Aid and WHMIS (Workplace Hazardous Materials Information System). Overall, the programme is designed to help members succeed, as it not only provides academic support, but also financial, emotional, social and cultural support. Another programme that is available to assist First Nations people with skills upgrading is the Nishnawbe Education and Training (NEAT) programme.

The Nishnawbe Education and Training (NEAT) programme, formerly known as the Ring of Fire Aboriginal Training Alliance (RoFATA), is a partnership between Confederation College, Noront and KKETS. The programme provides training for employment opportunities surrounding the mining industry for the Matawa First Nations community members. This initiative offers training through 12 skills upgrading programmes, categorized under Tier 1, Tier 2 and Tier 3 programmes. The training programmes range from Mining Essentials, Basic Line Cutting, Kitchen Helper, Remote Camp Supporter, Heavy Equipment Operator, Construction Craft Worker, Pre-Trades Welder, and many more (KKETS, 2017).

Under the NEAT partnership, a community member looking to upgrade their skills can enrol in the mentorship programme offered by Noront Resources. In this post-employment programme, a member is paired with an experienced worker to further refine skills and hone the tools necessary to excel in the occupation. The hands-on training is a key factor of success, as members not only get first-hand training from an experienced member in the industry, but also get an opportunity to strengthen their life skills such as workplace etiquette, including punctuality, dressing for work conditions, or following safety protocols. Apart from labour market and skills upgrading challenges, communities also face many economic development challenges that hinder their success in obtaining jobs.

Lack of resources, especially comparable funding, results in disparity in the quality of education that is provided in Matawa First Nations communities compared to more urban Northern Ontario communities. Notably, there is a gap in terms of delivery in First Nations education between federal (on-reserve) and provincial (off-reserve) education levels. Thus, when First Nations people leave to attend schools outside of their communities, they are routinely found to be producing work at a lower level than a non-Indigenous student of the same age and grade would normally be able to deliver. Education is the foundation for the strong economic viability of a nation. Despite that being the case, many First Nations students do not complete high school education, because it is simply not offered on-reserve and their families elect not to send their children away to complete secondary schooling. On the other hand, the reality is that most families anywhere would be reluctant to send their children away for years to school. The key issue is the lack of resources and lack of access to schools within Indigenous communities, which has created a serious inequity/divide between Indigenous and non-Indigenous communities.

Furthermore, many First Nations communities are small and rural; as a result there is a challenge of finding qualified teachers who are willing to go into the communities to teach. This limited pool of available teachers puts Indigenous People at a disadvantage as they do not get the same opportunities as those residing in urban centres to develop diverse and robust basic skills. It is important to note that provisions for education and other matters to rural and remote First Nation communities will cost far more than provisions for urban communities. Not expending those resources has a greater cost in limiting those populations from pursuing further post-secondary education. The inability for First Nations youth to attain the necessary and equal basic level of secondary education has a profoundly negative effect on the overall economy, as individuals cannot enter and flourish in a competitive post-secondary education system with a sub-competitive skill set.

To address that barrier, the ASAP programme offers a foundation credit course to help students fill those learning gaps. Unfortunately, many community members still struggle as they have been out of school for a long time, which adds additional obstacles for them to learn and grasp the new information. To help address their concerns, KKETS often hires extra help to assist students one-on-one.

MAWIW Council

Access to education and lack of educational qualifications are significant barriers for Indigenous People to achieve labour market success in New Brunswick. Working in partnership with Joint Economic Development Initiative (JEDI), the MAWIW Council constantly collaborates on how to effectively deliver services to its First Nations communities. Programmes and services provided by the Joint Economic Development Initiative (JEDI) and the community economic development office attempt to tackle these obstacles.

JEDI focused its workforce development efforts through the New Brunswick Aboriginal Information and Communications Technology (NBAICT) project, which was partially funded by ESDC through the Skills and Partnerships Fund from June 2011 to March 2017 JEDI served 380 total clients of which 94 were employed at the end of the intervention and 12 returned to school. Completed courses included: Apprenticeship, Security Training, Archaeology Field Technician training, Trades orientation, Workplace Essential Skills and Worksite Safety courses. In addition, JEDI partnered with CCNB and Rasakti to train 10 Indigenous machinists. The current students will be offered employment with Rasakti at the end of their training and 10 additional machinists are expected to begin training in January 2018 (Joint Economic Development Intiative , 2018)

The success of the programme is due to JEDI's strong partnership with Professional Quality Assurance and its sister company PLATO (Professional Aboriginal Testing Organization). The fully-accredited software tester training course has received great interest from Indigenous People across New Brunswick and has resulted in over 40 of the graduates working in full-time positions with PLATO Testing in Fredericton and Miramichi. This training will continue on for the next four years under the Indigenous Innovation Partnership Program (IIP) which is supported through SPF funding. JEDI has also offered programmes to Indigenous learners in the emerging and growing Information, Communications and Technology (ICT) sector in New Brunswick (see Box 2.1).

Box 2.1. ICT Training of Indigenous Learners using big data

The New Brunswick Aboriginal Information and Communications Technology project recruited Indigenous learners to take advanced ICT training in Big Data/Data Mining. These students graduated in June 2017. The Big Data/Data Mining programme is the result of funding received by the Collège communautaire du Nouveau Brunswick (CCNB) in partnership with the Indigenous and Northern Affairs Canada's Post-Secondary Partnership Program. NBAICT managed this project for CCNB including the recruitment and selection of students, coordination, delivery of the fully accredited 62-week programme, and the creation of an online version of the Big Data/Data Mining programme

Source: Joint Economic Development Initiative (2018), Annual Report 2016-17.

Critical success factors identified from the case studies

Looking across the four case study areas, the following key lessons emerge regarding the implementation of Indigenous skills development programmes at the local level:

Providing supports through the life-cycle

All case study areas highlighted the importance of getting Indigenous youth off to the right start. This means ensuring a robust continuum of support from cradle to grave. Across the case study areas, there was clear need expressed for more resources for child care and early childhood education programmes. More resources are required to support the development of child care spaces, create child care facilities and infrastructure as well as address issues related to the recruitment and training of staff. This is a key issue both in supporting potentially unemployed Indigenous adults who often require child care and early childhood education support to participate in the labour market but also as a tool to mentor children about the benefits of education.

Improve educational pathways from high-school into postsecondary skills training

It is important to build stronger and clear pathways from high-school into postsecondary education (e.g. college and university). Better targeting Indigenous youth with career guidance, wrap-around supports (books, transportation back home during holidays, spending money) and labour market information is critical and supporting them to find quality job opportunities. Often, ISET can fill the gap by providing support for Indigenous People to go to postsecondary education. Indigenous students often require customised and catered supports to complete their studies therefore, it would be important to examine how ISET programmes could possibly be designed in the future to support the transition from high school to postsecondary education.

Addressing employment barriers

Indigenous People often face multiple barriers to employment and may require intensive pre-employment supports. This includes literacy and basic skills training, personal coaching and mentoring, as well as other supports, such as support with transportation to work (e.g. public transportation tickets or subsidies). During the case study interviews, agreement holders noted that they face significant pressure to respond to the demand for services and supports. These types of "wrap-around" supports are important to consider in the context of Indigenous active labour market programmes.

Injecting additional flexibility within the management of vocational education and training policies

OECD research has highlighted the benefits of a flexible vocational education and training system, which enables programmes and courses to be agile and customised to meet the needs of the local labour market (OECD, 2017b). Close partnerships between ISET agreement holders and community colleges can help provide targeted skills development opportunities for Indigenous People. To support this, community colleges could further explore opportunities to design and deliver tailored programmes to the needs of Indigenous learners. A good example concerns the work of the Aboriginal Centre for Human Resource Development (CAHRD) who partnered with Red River Community College to offer a 10 month training programme to its Indigenous learners. Usually, training programmes are of a short-term nature at around 8 weeks.

Employer engagement in providing work experience

While both ISET and SPF are geared towards partnerships, there is a clear need to better engage employers locally to ensure that skills development programmes are well aligned to demand. The Centre for Aboriginal Human Resources and Development is an innovative example as training programmes were organised directly in partnership with local employers who are able to offer some of the Indigenous People high quality and high productive jobs following the training period. This report has already highlighted the need to develop better labour market information (LMI). Better LMI can also assist in identifying emerging job opportunities in which skills training programme could then be customised to Indigenous People. In many cases, Indigenous People do not have applicable labour market experience, making the transition to high quality employment more difficult. There is a need for stronger employer outreach mechanisms that would help to identify job vacancies but also work with employers to raise awareness about the benefits of employing Indigenous People. Some organisations have developed a cultural course that they present to employers to increase the understanding of the Indigenous population. Finding other partners in the community that can work with businesses is also fundamental to raise an awareness and understanding about human resources policies and practices for Indigenous People.

References

Joint Economic Development Intiative (2018), *Annual Report 2016-2017.*

KKETS (2017), *Employment & Training Services*, http://www.kkets.ca/ (accessed on 13 February 2018).

OECD (2017a), *Promising Practices in Supporting Success for Indigenous Students*, OECD Publishing, Paris, http://dx.doi.org/10.1787/9789264279421-en.

OECD (2017b), *Engaging Employers in Apprenticeship Opportunities: Making It Happen Locally*, OECD Publishing, http://dx.doi.org/10.1787/9789264266681-en.

OECD (2017c), *Policies for Stronger and More Inclusive Growth in Canada*, Better Policies, OECD Publishing, Paris, http://dx.doi.org/10.1787/9789264277946-en.

OECD (2017d), *Starting Strong 2017: Key OECD Indicators on Early Childhood Education and Care*, OECD Publishing, Paris, http://dx.doi.org/10.1787/9789264276116-en.

Shead, W. (2011), Cora J. Voyageur (ed.), *Dream and Today's Reality: Aboriginal Centre of Winnipeg - Adapting to Urban Life in Canada*, University of Toronto Press.

Statistics Canada (2012), International Survey of Adults, Programme for the International Assessment of Adult Competencies.

Statistics Canada (2015), *Aboriginal Statistics at a Glance: 2nd Edition*, http://www.statcan.gc.ca/pub/89-645-x/89-645-x2015001-eng.pdf (accessed on 10 July 2017).

Statistics Canada (2016a), 2016 Census, Statistics Canada Catalogue no. 98-400-X2016262.

Statistics Canada (2016b), 2016 Census, Catalogue Number 98-400-X2016267.

Statistics Canada (2016c), 2016 Census of Population. Canada and census metropolitan areas and census agglomerations, 2016 Census – 25% Sample data, data extracted by Employment and Skills Development Canada, received 11 April 2018.

The Conference Board of Canada - Northern and Aboriginal Policy (2017), *Opportunities to improve the financial ecosystem for Aboriginal entrepreneurs and SMEs in Canada*, NACCA and BDC, http://nacca.ca/wp-content/uploads/2017/04/ProjectSummary_NACCA-BDC_Feb14_2017.pdf.

Truth and Reconciliation Commission of Canada (2015), *Truth and Reconciliation Commission of Canada: Calls to Action*, Truth and Reconciliation Commission of Canada, Winnipeg, http://www.trc.ca/websites/trcinstitution/File/2015/Findings/Calls_to_Action_English2.pdf (accessed on 30 October 2017).

United Nations (2008), *United Nations Declaration on the Rights of Indigenous Peoples*, United Nations, http://www.un.org/esa/socdev/unpfii/documents/DRIPS_en.pdf (accessed on 23 October 2017).

Chapter 3. Indigenous job creation through SMEs and entrepreneurship policies

Attracting inward investments into Indigenous communities require a clear investment environment as well as incentives for businesses to locate in a region. This requires many communities to encourage entrepreneurship and provide business development support services. This chapter examines key trends in entrepreneurship and SME activity of Indigenous People and provides examples of programmes that have been implemented at the local level.

Fostering entrepreneurship opportunities for Indigenous People

As a young and growing demographic group, forecasts suggest that the Indigenous population could represent about one fifth of Canada's labour force growth over the next 20 years if gaps in the labour force participation rate were to close (Drummond, 2017). The provision of access to quality education and skills allows Indigenous People to ameliorate their participation in the labour force not only through increased employment and employee retention, but also through job creation as Indigenous entrepreneurs and SME owners—the Canadian Council for Aboriginal Business (CCAB) estimates that 36% of Indigenous businesses create further employment (Canadian Council for Aboriginal Business, 2016).

Self-employed Indigenous People boost the economy not only through their own employment and commerce, but often through the employment of other staff members as well. However, Indigenous People often confront barriers when seeking to become entrepreneurs—access to business financing, professional networks and financial literacy are issues that many Indigenous People have to address when considering the path of self-employment. While difficult, these adversities can be addressed and lead to thriving examples of Canadian enterprises both on and off reserve.

Current state of Indigenous entrepreneurship and SMEs in Canada

Similar to trends observed in the general Indigenous population, the numbers of Indigenous entrepreneurs in Canada is increasing substantially. According to the 2011 Canadian census, there were more than 37 000 Indigenous People self-employed in 2011[1]with nearly 10 000 Indigenous entrepreneurs entering the labour market from 2003 to 2011. In comparison with the 10.5% of non-Indigenous People who engage in self-employment, the 2011 NHS observes that 5.6% of Indigenous People were self-employed in 2011 (The Conference Board of Canada - Northern and Aboriginal Policy, 2017).

Indigenous businesses are also characterized as being profit and stability seeking (60%) in contrast to growth and risk (22%). Nearly two-thirds of Indigenous businesses have introduced new products, services or processes within three years of the survey, illustrating a prevalent culture of innovation and creativity (Canadian Council for Aboriginal Business, 2016). Additionally, the majority of Indigenous entrepreneurs' markets are focused within their local community area (Canadian Council for Aboriginal Business, 2016).

Mirroring the general population demographics, Indigenous entrepreneurs are considerably younger than their non-Indigenous counterparts. About 20% of Indigenous entrepreneurs are less than 25 years old, compared to 15% of non-Indigenous entrepreneurs. Therefore, organisations assisting Indigenous entrepreneurs may need to cater more services to a youthful market (The Conference Board of Canada – Northern and Aboriginal Policy, 2017).

Geographic location

At a provincial and territorial level, the majority of Indigenous entrepreneurs live in Alberta, British Columbia, Ontario and Quebec. According to CCAB, "self-employed Aboriginal people remain over represented in British Colombia and Alberta and underrepresented in Manitoba and Saskatchewan" compared to the total population in each area (Canadian Council for Aboriginal Business, 2016). At a regional level, the majority of Indigenous entrepreneurs are located off-reserve, with about 40% living in census metropolitan areas (SMA) of 100 000 people or more (DePratto, 2017) (The Conference Board of Canada – Northern and Aboriginal Policy, 2017). Furthermore, at a local level, most Indigenous businesses are home-based with two-thirds of self-employed entrepreneurs operating from their personal dwelling area (Canadian Council for Aboriginal Business, 2016). Of the on-reserve self-employed Indigenous population, 97% was comprised of First Nations people in 2011. Indigenous entrepreneurs on-reserve and in rural areas face additional challenges accessing larger markets and financial institutions. Some even have difficulties acquiring a bank account, let alone access to business loans. In contrast, Indigenous entrepreneurs living in an urban context have access to a larger market and network of resources. However, middle income Indigenous entrepreneurs may receive less attention from programme support while still facing a variety of structural and socioeconomic issues (The Conference Board of Canada – Northern and Aboriginal Policy, 2017).

Figure 3.1. Location of business, Reserve status, Aboriginal self-employed, %, 2011

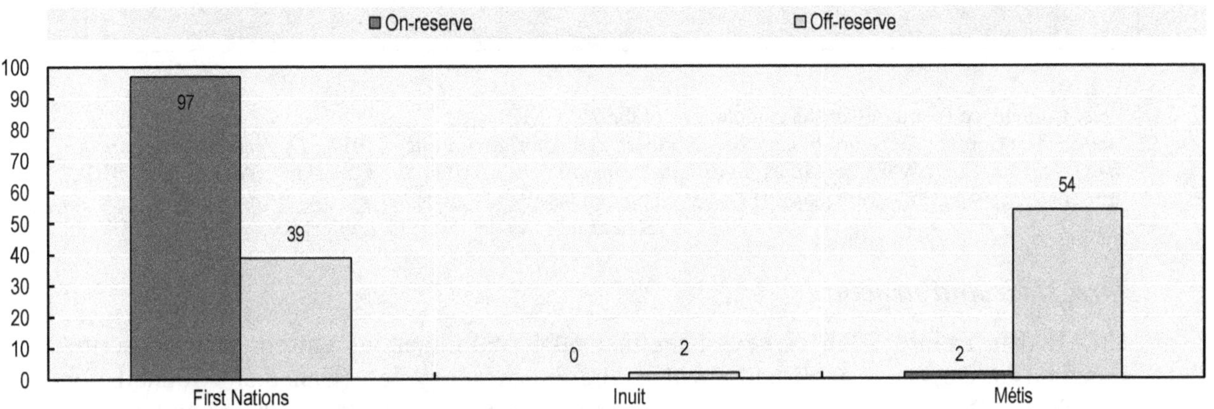

Note: Conference Board of Canada calculations of the 2011 NHS.

Source: The Conference Board of Canada - Northern and Aboriginal Policy (2017), *Opportunities to improve the financial ecosystem for Aboriginal entrepreneurs and SMEs in Canada*, NACCA and BDC, http://nacca.ca/wp-content/uploads/2017/04/ProjectSummary_NACCA-BDC_Feb14_2017.pdf.

StatLink http://dx.doi.org/10.1787/888933724119

Figure 3.2. Location of business, Geographic region, Indigenous self-employed, %, 2011

	Rural	Population centre
First Nations	34	42
Inuit	2	2
Métis	59	52

Note: Conference Board of Canada calculations of the 2011 NHS.
Source: The Conference Board of Canada - Northern and Aboriginal Policy (2017), *Opportunities to improve the financial ecosystem for Aboriginal entrepreneurs and SMEs in Canada*, NACCA and BDC, http://nacca.ca/wp-content/uploads/2017/04/ProjectSummary_NACCA-BDC_Feb14_2017.pdf.

StatLink http://dx.doi.org/10.1787/888933724138

Size, stage and structure

CCAB data from a 2016 survey states that 60% of Indigenous entrepreneurs describe their businesses as established (within the business cycle) (Canadian Council for Aboriginal Business, 2016). The same survey demonstrations that 73% of Indigenous business are unincorporated, with more than 60% of Indigenous businesses are sole proprietorships (Canadian Council for Aboriginal Business, 2016) (The Conference Board of Canada – Northern and Aboriginal Policy, 2017). These businesses provide to be easier to start in terms of structure and bureaucracy, but also, on-reserve entrepreneurs are further encouraged to use this model since corporations can still be taxed on reserves.

Within incorporated Indigenous businesses, there are Aboriginal Economic Development Corporations (AEDCs). About 260 are operating nationwide and the majority have less than 100 employees. While many are considered small businesses, they often have a large impact on their communities through employment. Furthermore, more than 66% of their employees are usually Indigenous People. AEDCs are normally owned by Indigenous governments, with a board of directors appointed by the Chief and Council and the local community as shareholders. These organisations are most prominently found in Ontario and within the industries of construction, energy, property management and tourism. In addition, AEDCs are more likely to use government funding to finance start-up costs rather than funds from personal savings or private businesses (The Conference Board of Canada – Northern and Aboriginal Policy, 2017).

Trends in Industries

Data from the Conference Board of Canada (2017) shows that Indigenous entrepreneurs are predominately found in the construction; professional, scientific and technical services; other services (except public administration); agriculture, forestry, fishing and hunting industries; and health care and social assistance. However, when comparing male and female entrepreneurs, Indigenous females most commonly work in healthcare and social assistance (18%) while Indigenous males most prevalently work in the construction industry (29.2 %) (The Conference Board of Canada - Northern and Aboriginal Policy, 2017). Furthermore, construction and agriculture, forestry, fishing and hunting were the two most common industries where Indigenous entrepreneurs worked in both on-reserve and in rural areas. At an urban level, the construction and professional, scientific, and technical services were the two top industries where Indigenous entrepreneurs worked. In general, Indigenous entrepreneurs are underrepresented in knowledge sectors and occupations while being overrepresented in the construction industry in particular (Canadian Council for Aboriginal Business, 2016).

Financing

For Indigenous People who do participate in self-employment, the main sources of financing for Indigenous entrepreneur are the National Aboriginal Capital Corporations Association (NACCA), Aboriginal Financial Institutions (AFIs), Business Development Bank of Canada (BDC), Indigenous Services Canada (ISC) and several major Canadian banks (The Conference Board of Canada - Northern and Aboriginal Policy, 2017). However, 65% of Indigenous entrepreneurs surveyed by CCAB stated that they started their business through the use of personal savings (Canadian Council for Aboriginal Business, 2016). Furthermore, only 14% of funding for Indigenous start-ups came from Indigenous lending institutions and 19% from bank or governmental financing. Therefore, some self-employed Indigenous People resort to finding business funding through the use of the personal savings of their family and social networks, credit cards, or revenues from multiple services (The Conference Board of Canada – Northern and Aboriginal Policy, 2017).

Figure 3.3. Sources of financing used to start-up businesses, %, 2015

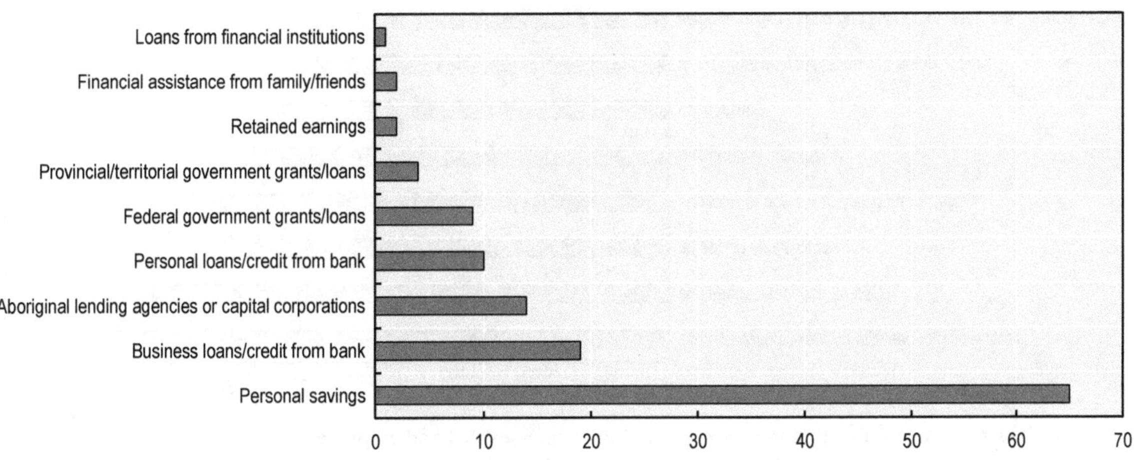

Note: The survey responses above were unprompted.
Source: Canadian Council for Aboriginal Business (2016), *Promise and Prosperity: the 2016 Aboriginal Business Survey*, https://www.ccab.com/wp-content/uploads/2016/10/CCAB-PP-Report-V2-SQ-Pages.pdf (accessed on 14 November 2017).

StatLink http://dx.doi.org/10.1787/888933724157

Future performance

A 2017 business survey shows that 77% of Canadians recognise the importance of thriving Indigenous enterprises for the creation of sustainable economic opportunities. (Sodexo, 2017). 76% of Indigenous entrepreneurs in the CCAB survey also observed net profits in 2015, a 15% increase from 2010 (Canadian Council for Aboriginal Business, 2016). A majority of Canadians also believed that supporting strong Indigenous businesses was an important pathway to healing Canada's relationship with First Nations, Inuit and Métis Peoples and non-Indigenous Canadians.

Which barriers are inhibiting the growth and sustainability of Indigenous entrepreneurs and SME owners?

Through the process of starting and managing their own companies, Indigenous entrepreneurs are often met with challenges. The Conference Board of Canada identified these issues as structural, financial, cultural and institutional barriers (The Conference Board of Canada – Northern and Aboriginal Policy, 2017). However, while some barriers remain as significant adversities, like the economic environment for Indigenous entrepreneurs, others can be more easily addressed. Respondents in the CCAB survey stated that while they anticipate several barriers to successful operations, infrastructure is of least concern (Canadian Council for Aboriginal Business, 2016). Through greater understanding of each issue, these barriers can be addressed more suitably.

Figure 3.4. Obstacles to business growth (over the next two years), %, 2015

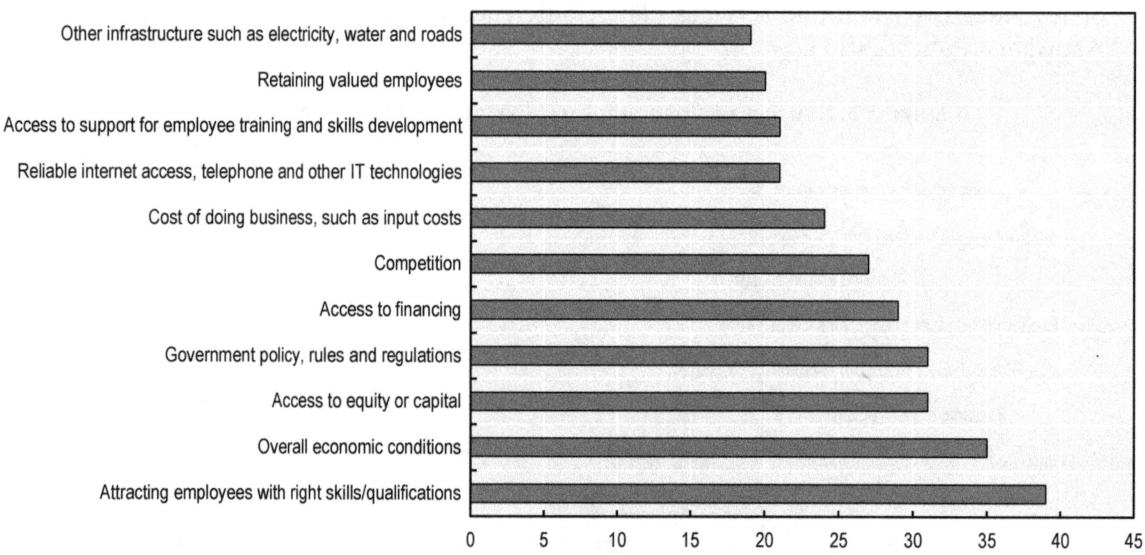

Note: Questions regarding employees were asked to businesses that had employees.

Source: Canadian Council for Aboriginal Business (2016), *Promise and Prosperity: the 2016 Aboriginal Business Survey*, https://www.ccab.com/wp-content/uploads/2016/10/CCAB-PP-Report-V2-SQ-Pages.pdf (accessed on 14 November 2017).

StatLink http://dx.doi.org/10.1787/888933724176

Financial barriers

Access to capital/equity

Despite the aforementioned avenues for financing, personal savings are often used to fund the majority of Indigenous businesses. Moreover, loans or credits from banks or government programmes are not used by a majority of Indigenous entrepreneurs (The Conference Board of Canada – Northern and Aboriginal Policy, 2017). CCAB data found 56% of Indigenous businesses had difficulty accessing capital for reason such as "a lack of collateral (8%); being a new, high-risks business (8%); having too much debt or poor credit rating (8%); dealing with bureaucracy (8%); and being Aboriginal (7%)" (The Conference Board of Canada - Northern and Aboriginal Policy, 2017).

While prevalent, sole proprietorship businesses can often be labelled as high risk and have difficulties lending from banks. Indigenous sole proprieties on-reserve have some benefits, like protection from banks seizing property due to the *Indian Act*. However, this in turn makes it difficult for them to receive loans since they may not have other assets to offer as collateral. Furthermore, start-up, poor credit ratings, high debt, socio-economic disadvantages, and discrimination can often add to Indigenous sole-proprietors' label as high-risk in the eyes of leaders (The Conference Board of Canada – Northern and Aboriginal Policy, 2017).

Education, financial literacy and capacity

As demonstrated in the previous chapter, there are substantial gaps between Indigenous and non-Indigenous education and skill outcomes. Furthermore, 68% of Indigenous entrepreneurs state that they have had difficulties finding qualified Indigenous employees (Canadian Council for Aboriginal Business, 2016). Financial literacy can be simply defined as knowledge of financial management. In comparison, financial capacity encapsulates both financial education and opportunities to participate in affordable and reliable financial products and services. The Conference Board of Canada states, "education, literacy, and numeracy challenges combined with the remote nature of many Aboriginal communities and their infrastructure deficits, all play a role in weakening financial literacy. In addition, Collin argues that 'cultural barriers such as language, values that affect financial decisions, the persistence of non-cash-based economies, lack of trust toward financial institutions, and habituation to government programme management culture of all affect financial literacy' for Aboriginal entrepreneurs" (The Conference Board of Canada – Northern and Aboriginal Policy, 2017).

Figure 3.5. Actively seek external advice or input for business, %, 2015

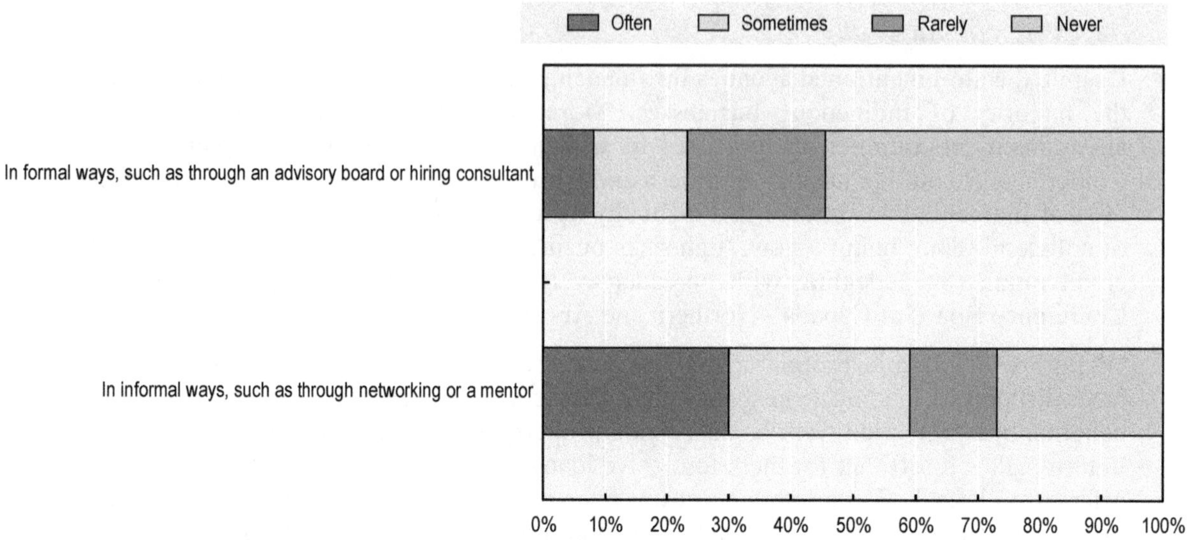

Source: Canadian Council for Aboriginal Business (2016), *Promise and Prosperity: the 2016 Aboriginal Business Survey*, https://www.ccab.com/wp-content/uploads/2016/10/CCAB-PP-Report-V2-SQ-Pages.pdf (accessed on 14 November 2017).

StatLink http://dx.doi.org/10.1787/888933724195

Many Indigenous businesses supply the market with a specialization in the product or service they provide. However, in regards to entrepreneurship and SMEs, less Indigenous People (20.7%) are trained in business and management in comparison to non-Indigenous People (26.8%) (Statistics Canada, 2018). For example, TD Economics reports that only 31% of Indigenous businesses have a formal business plan (DePratto, 2017). Therefore, in instances where Indigenous entrepreneurs lack business training, many of these businesses have the potential to generate more growth and profitability through supports from further education and training. For instance, the possession of a business plan has been correlated to innovation and growth within Indigenous businesses (DePratto, 2017).

Figure 3.6. Top reasons for not having a business plan, %, 2015

Among those without a business plan for the past year

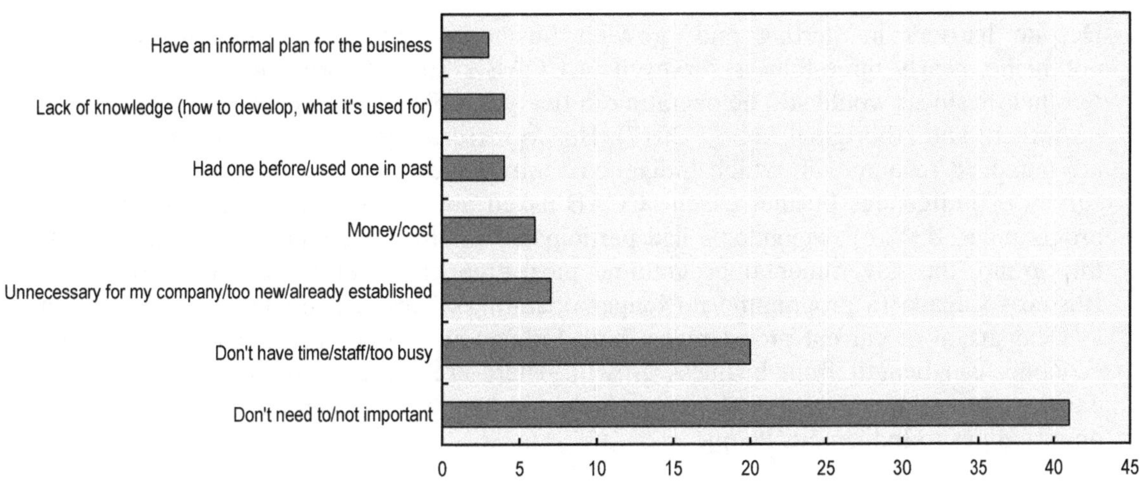

Note: Subsample: Businesses with no business plan (n=709)
Source: Canadian Council for Aboriginal Business (2016), *Promise and Prosperity: the 2016 Aboriginal Business Survey*, https://www.ccab.com/wp-content/uploads/2016/10/CCAB-PP-Report-V2-SQ-Pages.pdf (accessed on 14 November 2017).

StatLink http://dx.doi.org/10.1787/888933724214

Increases in fringe financial services

A lack of access to financial institutions combined with a deficiency in financial capacity have provided an environment for fringe financial services to expand in many Indigenous communities. Fringe financial services, or predatory lending, impact small-sized businesses in particular. The Conference Board of Canada states that "Predatory lending encompasses a wide variety of services, including but not limited to, pawnshops, payday lenders, and cheque cashers, all of which can be very expensive" (The Conference Board of Canada – Northern and Aboriginal Policy, 2017).

Geographic barriers impacting Indigenous entrepreneurs

Only 50 branches of major Canadian banks are located in Indigenous communities across Canada (the 50 branches are within the major Canadian banks, such as Bank of Montreal, Toronto Dominion Bank, CIBC, Royal Bank of Canada and Scotiabank). Some Indigenous communities have loan and support programmes. For example, Ulnooweg has been providing loans and business services to Aboriginal entrepreneurs in Atlantic Canada since 1986. However, in many rural communities, there are fewer and less diverse business opportunities compared to more urbanised places or cities with a larger population and stronger density of business activities" (The Conference Board of Canada – Northern and Aboriginal Policy, 2017).

TD Economics reported that a substantial amount of Indigenous businesses had difficulties with internet access (DePratto, 2017). The 2016 National Aboriginal Business Survey reported that 40% of Indigenous business owners either have no or unreliable internet access (Canadian Council for Aboriginal Business, 2016). This issue is partially related to geography and resources rural entrepreneurs can access (DePratto, 2017).

Which policies and programmes have been implemented to foster entrepreneurial and SME growth and sustainability for Indigenous People?

Despite barriers in starting and growing businesses, Indigenous entrepreneurs are optimistic, nearly three-fourths surveyed in CCAB's 2016 Aboriginal Business Survey felt their business would still be operating in five years (The Conference Board of Canada - Northern and Aboriginal Policy, 2017). But to increase growth and profitability, there are untapped resources in which Indigenous entrepreneurs can capitalise. In their 2016 survey of Indigenous businesses, the CCAB asked about participation in governmental programmes. 43% of respondents had participated in any governmental programme. Of this group, the governmental programme most frequently referenced was Aboriginal Business Canada (a programme no longer operating). Through greater access, creation and expansion of current programmes, both Indigenous entrepreneurs and the Canadian economy can benefit from business growth. There are some good examples below of existing programmes and policies, which aim to provide more entrepreneurship opportunities to Indigenous People.

Figure 3.7. Government programmes used (most frequent responses), %, 2015

Among businesses that have used any government programmes

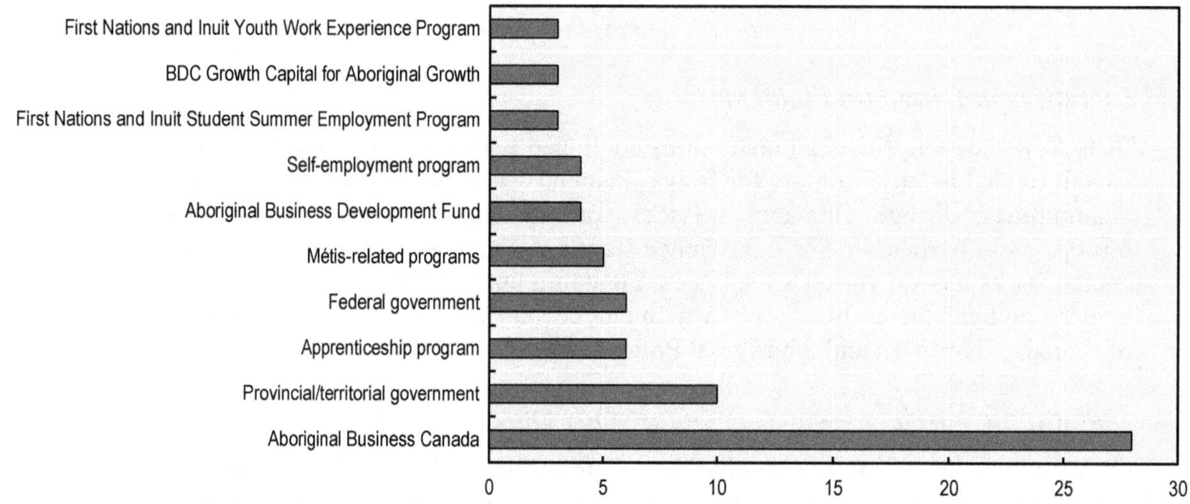

Note: The survey question was "Which government programs have you used?" This is a subsample: Ever used any government programs (n=514).

Source: Canadian Council for Aboriginal Business (2016), *Promise and Prosperity: the 2016 Aboriginal Business Survey*, https://www.ccab.com/wp-content/uploads/2016/10/CCAB-PP-Report-V2-SQ-Pages.pdf (accessed on 14 November 2017).

StatLink http://dx.doi.org/10.1787/888933724233

Figure 3.8. Reasons for not using government programmes, %, 2015

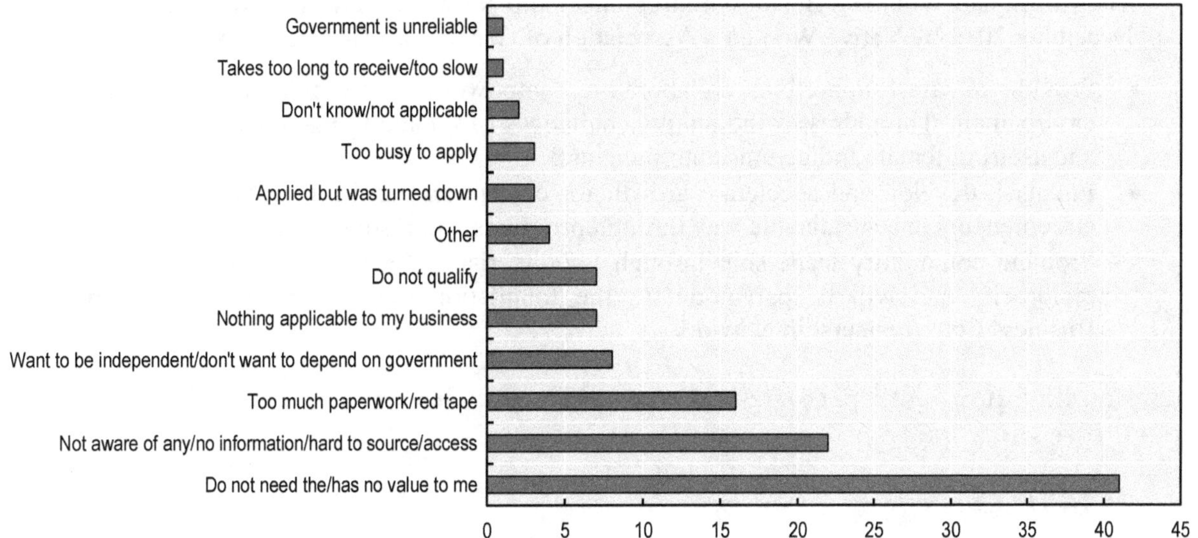

Note: The survey question was "What is the main reason why you have not used any government programs?" It is a subset: Never used any government programs (n=587).
Source: Canadian Council for Aboriginal Business (2016), *Promise and Prosperity: the 2016 Aboriginal Business Survey*, https://www.ccab.com/wp-content/uploads/2016/10/CCAB-PP-Report-V2-SQ-Pages.pdf (accessed on 14 November 2017).

StatLink http://dx.doi.org/10.1787/888933724252

First Nations Bank of Canada

The First Nations Bank of Canada is the first Canadian chartered bank to be independently controlled by Indigenous shareholders. The First Nations Bank of Canada provides financial services to Indigenous People and is an advocate for the growth of the Indigenous economy and the economic well-being of Indigenous People. The Bank aims to increase shareholder value by participating in and promoting the development of the Indigenous economy.

The Bank was conceived and developed by Indigenous People, for Indigenous People and regards itself as an important step toward Indigenous economic self-sufficiency. The strategic directive of the founding shareholders was to grow the Bank and increase Indigenous ownership to the point that the Bank would be controlled by a widely held group of Indigenous shareholders. The Bank is over 80% owned and controlled by Indigenous shareholders from Alberta, Saskatchewan, Manitoba, Yukon, Northwest Territories, Nunavut and Quebec (First Nations Bank of Canada, 2018).

The Canadian Centre for Aboriginal Entrepreneurship (CCAE)

The CCAE has assisted more than 75 business owners to start their new firm. CCAE provides entrepreneurship training, consultation services, speaking and writing services, and project management recommendations (Canadian Centre for Aboriginal Entrepreneurship, 2017). The Aboriginal Best (Business and Entrepreneurship Skills Training) programme of CCAE has worked with 95 Indigenous communities, including more than 2 000 participants (Canadian Centre for Aboriginal Entrepreneurship, 2017) (Aboriginal Business & Entrepreneurship Skills Training, 2018).

Aboriginal Women's Business Entrepreneurship Network

The Aboriginal Women's Business Entrepreneurship Network (AWBEN) was initiated in December 2012 by Native Women's Association of Canada. It was created to:

- Provide a safe, supportive, collaborative, empowering and culturally supportive environment that addresses the unique challenges of female Indigenous entrepreneurs and aspiring female Indigenous entrepreneurs;
- Enhance, develop and accelerate growth for current and aspiring female Indigenous entrepreneurs in a sustainable way through programs and resources, and
- Promote community leadership through volunteerism as a reflection of respect and reciprocity and will be paramount to the foundation of the Aboriginal Women's Business Entrepreneurship Network.

Understanding how entrepreneurship and SME policies are being implemented through case study analysis

MAWIW Council

Isolated First Nations communities face several barriers in pursuing economic development opportunities. The remoteness factor of communities' means limited outside traffic and this has a big impact on corporations wanting to invest in the area. This often limits diversity in economic development opportunities on Indigenous communities, as most organisations or businesses that come to town are related to mining. Thus, giving members limited employment choices. Secondly, politics plays a role in creating economic development opportunities, as Chiefs and Councils on-reserve serve two year terms. This presents a huge limitation as community leaders are unable to carry out long-term goals because they are constantly campaigning for a re-election. Though, there is a political shift happening in many communities to have four year terms for their leaders, it is not a reality in every community. This limits economic growth in MAWIW First Nations' communities. There are Economic Development Officers (EDOs) situated in each community to assist members with capacity development. These efforts are supported by JEDI, as they provide specific programmes and service to help individuals start up their own businesses.

On the other hand, MAWIW Council does not offer direct programmes for economic development or entrepreneurship programmes in their communities, as their primary focus is on providing employment and training services. However, JEDI works closely with all First Nations' communities to offer economic development and entrepreneurship services. One good example is the Business Incubator Program (see Box 3.1).

Box 3.1. Indigenous Business Incubator Program

Indigenous Business Incubator Program provides entrepreneurs with knowledge of business basics like preparing customized business plans, accessing funding and how to effectively market their products and services. In this 10 week programme which focuses on tourism, trades and technology, individuals can also receive mentorship from experienced entrepreneurs working in the same field. The Indigenous Business Accelerator Program on the other hand helps individuals gain business knowledge in the aerospace and defence industry, with employment in, Information Communication Technology (ICT), Industrial Manufacturing, Security, Clean Energy and Consulting. Participants of this programme also get access to key resources such as venture capital funds, research and development organisations and meeting with players in the industry (Joint Economic Development Initiative, 2018). Thus, community members are able to access entrepreneurship services through JEDI; however, with limited capacity, not everyone is able to take advantage of the programmes.

Community Futures Treaty Seven (CFT7)

In the area of entrepreneurship, CFT7 builds the Treaty Seven economy through community economic development and entrepreneur capacity building in order to assist and support Treaty Seven First Nations and their members towards economic success. This includes a general loan fund where loans are provided to establish or expand a business. In these cases, business must be at least 51% owned by Treaty Seven Members and the maximum loan per business is 25 000 CDN. All loans require equity of 10% (or proof of sweat equity) and they are provided to businesses located on and off-reserve. All loans require community support through a Band Council Resolution (on-reserve only) and there must be a business mandate to increase the employment of Treaty Seven Members over the long-term.

CFT7 has also a business development programme, which provides technical assistance to Indigenous entrepreneurs. This programme offers support to review business plans; assist in the creation & development of a business, counselling; identifying potential market opportunities; entrepreneurial training as well as small business workshops and entrepreneurial training available upon request.

CFT7 also operates First Nations Youth Entrepreneur Symposium which includes some team building and risk taking activities. This is an annual event and the symposium concludes with a banker’s panel in which participants present a draft business plan for feedback on how to improve and make the business plan bankable. Qualified trainers are usually onsite to assist with the development of the business plan.

Kiikenomaga Kikenjigewen Employment & Training Services (KKETS)

Related to the lack of education is the absence of business knowledge, which creates a barrier for entrepreneurial members of the community population that want to start up their own business. The ASAP programme offers an entrepreneur credit, an elective course to those who want to learn more about being an entrepreneur. The course teaches participants how to write a business plan and the major requirements of opening up a business. Due to funding limitations, KKETS does not offer any additional services or programmes for entrepreneurs where they can seek help as they go through the process of starting their own business.

The Centre for Aboriginal Human Resources and Development

CAHRD does not offer specific training related to entrepreneurship. In the past, business development programmes were offered by the Neeginan Centre under pilot funding but they were not continued. The Centre has created a social enterprise - Mother Earth Recycling, which has been operating under the auspices of Neeginan Centre and CAHRD (see Box 3.2).

Box 3.2. Indigenous Social Enterprises

Mother Earth Recycling (MER) is a Winnipeg-based Indigenous social enterprise. The goal of the social enterprise is to provide meaningful training and employment opportunities to the Indigenous community through environmentally sustainable initiatives. MER began in 2012 as a partnership between Neeginan Centre, the Centre for Aboriginal Human Resource Development, and the Aboriginal Council of Winnipeg, as a place for community members to find training and job opportunities, while providing a much-needed service to the City. MER offers mattress, box springs, and e-waste pickup and drop off from residential homes, businesses, and industries across Manitoba. Part of the early success of MER is due to its innovative collaboration and partnerships. The owners and all three levels (e.g. municipal, provincial and federal) of government have invested resources in the development of MER. Public participation and support have also greatly contributed to its success. The act of recycling has cultural significance for Indigenous communities in Canada. Embedded within traditional Indigenous worldviews is the concept of collective responsibility to respect and maintain the natural environment, and use only what is needed for sustenance. The commitment to environmental sustainability enables Indigenous employees to reconnect with an integral part of their culture.

Critical success factors identified from the case studies

Evidences of entrepreneurial best practices were present throughout the case studies examined in this report. These examples of successful Indigenous enterprises in turn provide helpful lessons for continued success among all Indigenous businesses. Many of case studies looked to changes in both financial institutions and entrepreneurial education as areas that can improve to produce even higher results.

Making financial capital more accessible

The case studies' showed that financial institutions and Indigenous entrepreneurs appear to be disconnected in regards to financial capital. With 65% of Indigenous entrepreneurs using their personal savings as funding, financial institutions have ample room for growth in their support for Indigenous businesses (Canadian Council for Aboriginal Business, 2016). When Indigenous entrepreneurs have better access to loans and credit, more jobs can be created through new enterprises and maintained through stable finances (The Conference Board of Canada, 2017).

While several financial institutions would like to lend to more self-employed Indigenous People, poor credit scores can prevents some entrepreneurs from participating. Considering funding barriers, alternative financing can be found through a greater use of micro loans. The amounts lent would be smaller and easier to manage, allowing Indigenous borrowers to consistently increase their credit ratings. Additionally, credit building programmes also offer ways to allow Indigenous entrepreneurs to change their credit ratings in a structured and accountable environment (The Conference Board of Canada, 2017).

Furthermore, more funds could be allocated to Aboriginal Financial Institutions (AFIs) to support more start-up ventures and to support the growth of more mature ventures as well. Currently only 22% of Indigenous businesses survey stated that they were seeking further growth and expansion (Canadian Council for Aboriginal Business, 2016). The number of Indigenous businesses that could move into positions of growth and expansion could rise dramatically if they had reliable and more extensive funds beyond their personal savings. The profits from these companies could in turn boost their local, regional and national economy.

Closing financial literacy and capacity gaps

With increases in access to financial capital, case studies indicated that there should be equal attention given towards the education of Indigenous borrowers in financial literacy and capacity. In particular, there are gaps in participation and outcomes for some groups of Indigenous entrepreneurs, such as youth and women, which show that they need even further support. These educational initiatives can allow Indigenous entrepreneurs the ability to make the most of their new resources.

One of the easiest ways to target Indigenous entrepreneurs seeking financial capital is to attach financial literacy and capacity education to lending requirements. Banks and other financial institutions can work with local stakeholders to create programmes highly relevant to Indigenous borrowers. These programmes would protect the credit rating of Indigenous entrepreneurs while also reducing risks in noncompliance of loan repayments (The Conference Board of Canada, 2017).

While there are still fewer women entrepreneurs compared to men, a large portion are women. Women entrepreneurs also report requiring fewer funds to start their business. Therefore, micro-lending could be a beneficial solution to their business needs in some cases. However, Métis Financial Institutions report that micro lending can sometimes be more of a burden than the funds are worth in terms of administrative requirements. Therefore, women should be educated about the benefits and disadvantages of each option to select the most appropriate method needed to finance their businesses (The Conference Board of Canada, 2017).

With one fifth of Indigenous entrepreneurs less than 25 years old (compared to on 15% of non-Indigenous entrepreneurs), financial institutions need to prepare their programming and educational services to be marketed to younger audiences as well. With far less experience managing personal funds as well, these entrepreneurs will need to be exposed to holistic financial literacy and capacity training to ensure that they have been exposed to all aspects of financial management. Finally, these entrepreneurs may need additional assistance meeting additionally requirements needed when applying for loans or credit (The Conference Board of Canada, 2017).

Note

1. However, the population of Indigenous entrepreneurs recorded by the 2011 NHS possibly underestimates the number of on-reserve entrepreneurs. The 2015 Canadian Business Patterns (CBP) data from the Statistics Canada Business Register shows 10 000 businesses located on-reserve (compared to 3 000 captured by the 2011 NHS) (The Conference Board of Canada – Northern and Aboriginal Policy, 2017). Moreover, TD Economics reported that about 2% of registered SMEs in Canada (e.g. around 32 000 businesses) were owned by Indigenous People (DePratto, 2017). Due to different sources and metrics for measuring the presence of Indigenous entrepreneurs and SME owners, it is difficult to obtain a consistent figure on the prevalence of Indigenous businesses in Canada.

References

Aboriginal Business & Entrepreneurship Skills Training (2018), *Aboriginal Entrepreneurship & Business Skills Training*, http://aboriginalbest.com/ (accessed on 13 February 2018).

Canadian Centre for Aboriginal Entrepreneurship(2017) *Aboriginal BEST*, http://www.ccae.ca/aboriginal-best/ (accessed on 23 October 2017).

Canadian Council for Aboriginal Business (2016), *Promise and Prosperity: the 2016 Aboriginal Business Survey*, https://www.ccab.com/wp-content/uploads/2016/10/CCAB-PP-Report-V2-SQ-Pages.pdf (accessed on 14 November 2017).

DePratto, B. (2017), *Aboriginal Businesses Increasingly Embracing Innovation*, TD Economics, https://www.td.com/document/PDF/economics/special/AboriginalBusiness2017.pdf (accessed on 19 October 2017).

Drummond, A. (2017), *The Contribution of Aboriginal People to Future Labour Force Growth in Canada*, Centre for the Study of Living Standards.

Joint Economic Development Intiative (2018), *Annual Report 2016-2017*.

Statistics Canada (2011), *Calculations based on Public Use Microdata File*, http://www12.statcan.gc.ca/nhs-enm/2011/dp-pd/pumf-fmgd/index-eng.cfm.

The Conference Board of Canada - Northern and Aboriginal Policy (2017), *Opportunities to improve the financial ecosystem for Aboriginal entrepreneurs and SMEs in Canada*, NACCA and BDC, http://nacca.ca/wp-content/uploads/2017/04/ProjectSummary_NACCA-BDC_Feb14_2017.pdf.

Chapter 4. Urban Indigenous People in Canada

Indigenous People in Canada often live and work in urban settings. Over the last decade, there has been a strong trend towards the urbanisation of Indigenous People. In some cities, such as Winnipeg and Thunder Bay, the Indigenous population represents a significant segment of the labour market and local economy. This chapter outlines the key role played by local governments in Canada in delivering Indigenous services. It also outlines several initiatives and examples of programmes and policies targeted to urban Indigenous People.

Local government in Canada

Municipal governments in Canada

Municipal governments in Canada constitute a local government unit, which is often responsible for delivering a range of public services. Municipal governments in Canada are largely accountable to their respective province. While municipal governments are highly varied across Canada, the recent trend has seen many provinces and territories introducing legislation and regulation to give them more autonomy in how they deliver services and programmes. Relative to other OECD countries, the number of municipal government units in Canada is significantly less than that of the United States, Germany, and Spain (other countries, which are federations), partially due to a lower population. In 2015, there were 3 945 municipal government units across Canada. This is higher than countries, such as Mexico (2 458), Switzerland (2 225), Austria (2 122), Belgium (589), and Australia (563).

Figure 4.1. Number of municipal government units, selected OECD countries, 2015

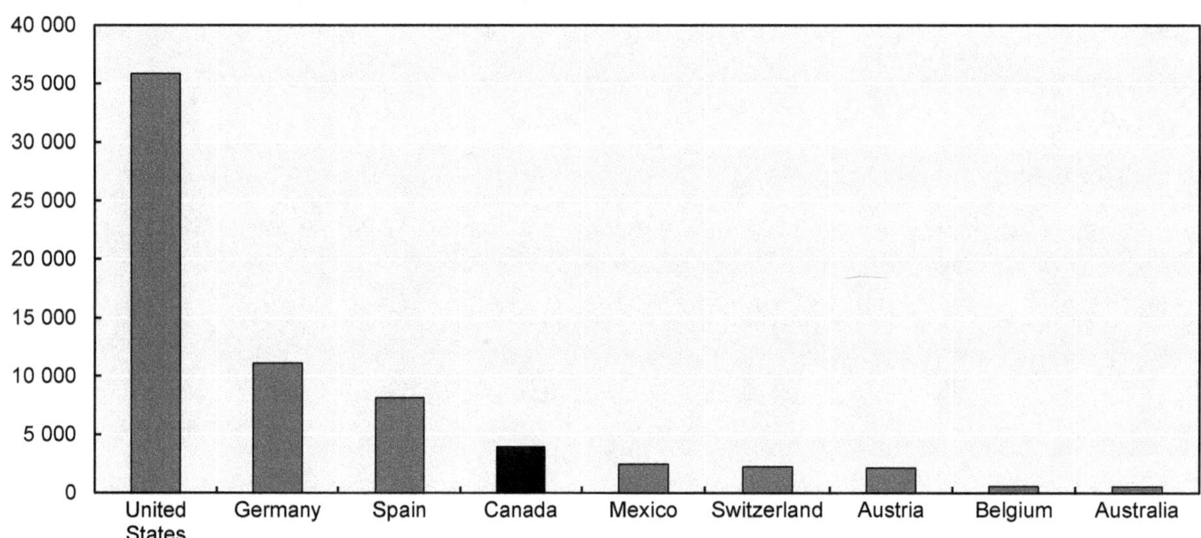

Source: OECD (2018), "Subnational government structure and finance", OECD Regional Statistics (database).

StatLink http://dx.doi.org/10.1787/888933724271

Urban development policies

In terms of fostering Indigenous, non-Indigenous and governmental partnerships within an urban context, Canada does not currently have a national urban policy in place. Therefore, policies concerning urban development are designed through national sectorial and subnational policies. Currently, the exchange of information and ideas between governing bodies occurs regularly within First Ministers Meetings or Conferences (FMMs). The stakeholders included in these meetings include federal, territorial and provincial representatives. However, other councils have developed to contribute to these efforts. In addition, Regional Development Agencies (RDAs) and Innovation, Science, and Economic Development Canada (ISED) have roles in regional economic development which include regional policy advocacy at the national level, collecting local economic data, increasing foreign investment, and boosting innovation (OECD, 2017).

However, historically, Canada had several national frameworks on urban policy. In 1995 Urban Development Agreements were created (however, they were all discontinued by 2010). Not long after the creation of Urban Development Agreements, an Urban Aboriginal Strategy was established in 1997 by Indigenous and Northern Affairs Canada seeking to improve the integration of Indigenous People within metropolitan areas. In 2001, the Caucus Task Force on Urban Issues gave recommendations which further developed infrastructure policies. Although, the Task Force's "suggestion of an urban ministry was rejected because cities are under the responsibility of provinces [and territories]" (OECD, 2017). In 2003, a Cities Secretariat was formed and later merged within Infrastructure Canada. Finally, New Deals for cities and communities were implemented in 2004-2005. "The objectives were to ensure predictable long-term funding for communities of all sizes, provide more effective programme support for infrastructure and social priorities, give communities a stronger voice, and to improve the co-operation between federal, provincial, territorial and municipal governments" (OECD, 2017). In return for these new rights, cities acquired new responsibilities in terms of taxes and transfers (OECD, 2017).

Current mechanisms influencing urban policy

The nationwide bodies that work on issues relating to urban development reside within the economic, housing, infrastructure and monetary sectors. In particular, Canada Mortgage and Housing Corporation, the Gas Tax Fund and Infrastructure Canada act as key bodies that shape policies and funding of urban development. Additionally, funding for urban infrastructure is included in the 2016 national budget plan. Specifically this includes "investments in public transit, waste and wastewater services, and affordable housing" (OECD, 2017). In the same year, premiers from Alberta, British Columbia, Nova Scotia and Quebec pledged support to new infrastructure agreements for public transit and water as well (OECD, 2017).

The evolution of municipal powers

The distribution of powers to municipal government is slowly evolving. For instance, the City of Toronto Act of 2006 has widened the general powers of the Canada's largest city. Seeing the need for more harmonized design and implementation of policies, the City of Toronto Act was created to give the municipality more autonomy in managing its jurisdiction. While the province of Ontario still has jurisdiction in Toronto, the Act of Toronto recognizes that the city has local knowledge and legitimate authority in managing itself regarding several issues (Ontario Ministry of Municipal Affairs, 2018).

While municipal powers are evolving in Canada, municipal governments do not have the same level of financial capacity and resources as local governments in countries, such as Sweden, Finland, and the United States. Spending by local governments made up 8.7% of Canadian GDP in 2015; while the average among OECD countries was 16.4% (see Figure 4.2).

Figure 4.2. Total expenditure incurred by local levels of government as a percentage of GDP, 2015

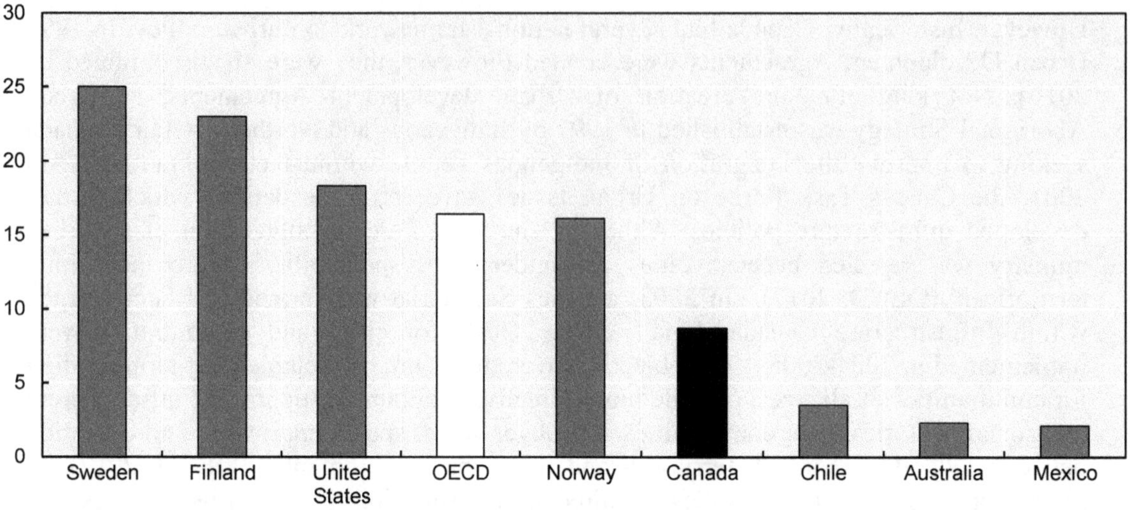

Source: OECD (2018), "Subnational government structure and finance", OECD Regional Statistics (database).

Note: Values for Chile, Finland, Norway; Sweden and the United States correspond to sub-national (rather than local) levels of government.

StatLink http://dx.doi.org/10.1787/888933724290

Box 4.1. More responsibility and autonomy for Canada's two largest cities

The move to give cities more responsibility in the management of policies and programmes is exemplified in the City of Toronto Act as well as move to establish the City of Montreal as Metropolis.

In the Province of Ontario, on January 1, 2007 the City of Toronto Act, 2006 came into force, setting out a broad, permissive legislative framework for the city that gives it more tools commensurate with its size, responsibilities and significance. The City of Toronto Act brings about a legislative framework for Toronto that balances the interests of the province and the city. Toronto's council is now better able to respond to the city's needs.

The city has broad powers to pass by-laws on matters ranging from health and safety to the city's economic, social and environmental well-being, subject to certain limitations. City by-laws can better deal with the financial management of Toronto and the accountability and transparency of its operations.

The act helps to ensure that the city is accountable to the public and that the processes for making decisions are transparent. The City is better able to determine the appropriate mechanisms for delivering municipal services, determine the appropriate levels of municipal spending, and use fiscal tools to support the city's activities.

In Quebec, Bill 121 has been introduced which grants Montreal the status of "metropolis". This legislation provides new fiscal and regulatory powers to the City, as well as an ability to grant direct subsidies and tax credits to attract inward investments.

Source: Ontario Ministry of Municipal Affairs (2018), available at http://www.mah.gov.on.ca/Page343.aspx; National Assembly Quebec (2017),"An Act to increase the autonomy powers of Ville de Montréal", Québec, available at http://www2.publicationsduquebec.gouv.qc.ca/dynamicSearch/telecharge.php?type=5&file=2017C16A.PDF.

Understanding Canada's urban Indigenous population

Urban Indigenous People

The term urban Indigenous People refers primarily to First Nation, Inuit, and Métis individuals currently residing in CMAs. It is critical to look at urban policy setting when analysing the employment and economic development outcomes of Indigenous People in Canada because the off-reserve population is the fastest growing segment of Canadian society (Indigeneous and Northern Affairs Canada, 2018). According to Statistics Canada, in 2016, 867 415 Indigenous People lived in a metropolitan area of at least 30 000 people, accounting for over half (51.8%) of the total Indigenous population. From 2006 to 2016, the number of Indigenous People living in a metropolitan area of this size increased by 59.7% (Statistics Canada, 2017a). This urbanisation is due to multiple factors—including demographic growth, mobility and changing patterns of self-reported identity.

Urban Indigenous People population trends

At an urban level, the largest population of Indigenous Canadians reported in the 2016 Census is found in Winnipeg (92 810 persons). However, the largest population percent distribution of Indigenous People in a census metropolitan area (CMA) in the 2016

Census is 12.7% in Thunder Bay. After Thunder Bay, Winnipeg has the second highest percentage of Indigenous People within the population at 12.2% (Statistics Canada, 2017b).

Figure 4.3. Indigenous populations per CMA, Population Count, 2011 and 2016

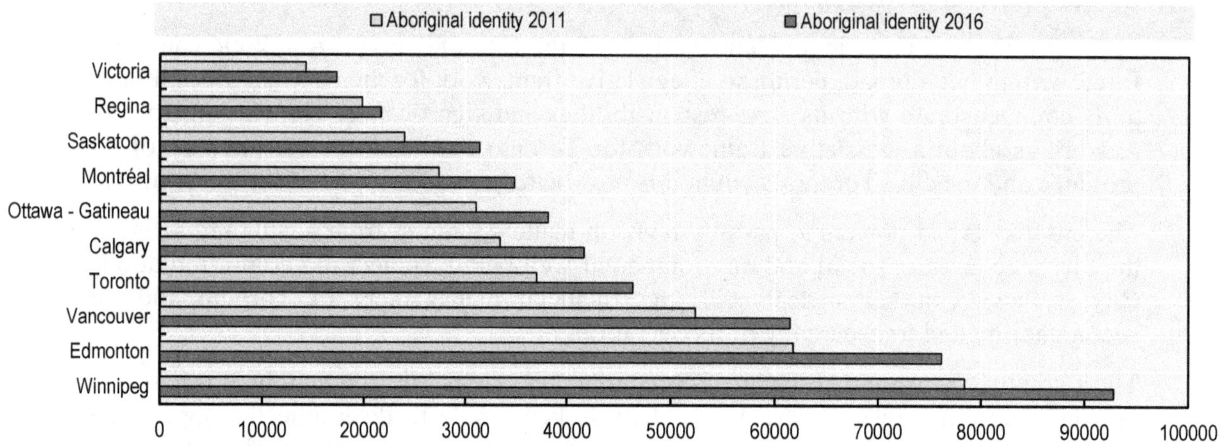

Note: Only the 2016 counts provided in this table are unadjusted. Therefore, the 2016 Census counts are not based on adjusted counts for the incompletely enumerated Indian reserves and Indian settlements of previous census years, while the percentage change is based on adjusted counts.
Source: Statistics Canada (2016) 2016 Census of Population. Aboriginal identity population by both sexes, total - age, 2016 counts, Canada and census metropolitan areas and census agglomerations, 2016 Census – 25% Sample data, Statistics Canada Catalogue no. 98-402-X2016009. Ottawa. Released 25 October 2017. http://www12.statcan.gc.ca/census-recensement/2016/dp-pd/hlt-fst/aboaut/Table.cfm?Lang=Eng&T=102&S=102&O=D&RPP=9999.

StatLink http://dx.doi.org/10.1787/888933724309

Figure 4.4 shows the change in the distribution of the Indigenous population within Canada's largest cities from 2011-16. One can see that in all of Canada's largest cities (except for Regina), the percentage of the population reporting Indigenous identity increased relative to the overall city population. This increase was particularly pronounced in Winnipeg and Thunder Bay; however even larger cities such as Toronto, Montreal and Vancouver saw an increase in the percentage of the overall population reporting Indigenous identity. In Winnipeg, the Indigenous population has reached nearly 92 810 – more than four times higher than it was 25 years earlier.

Figure 4.4. Indigenous populations per CMA, population % distribution, 2011 and 2016

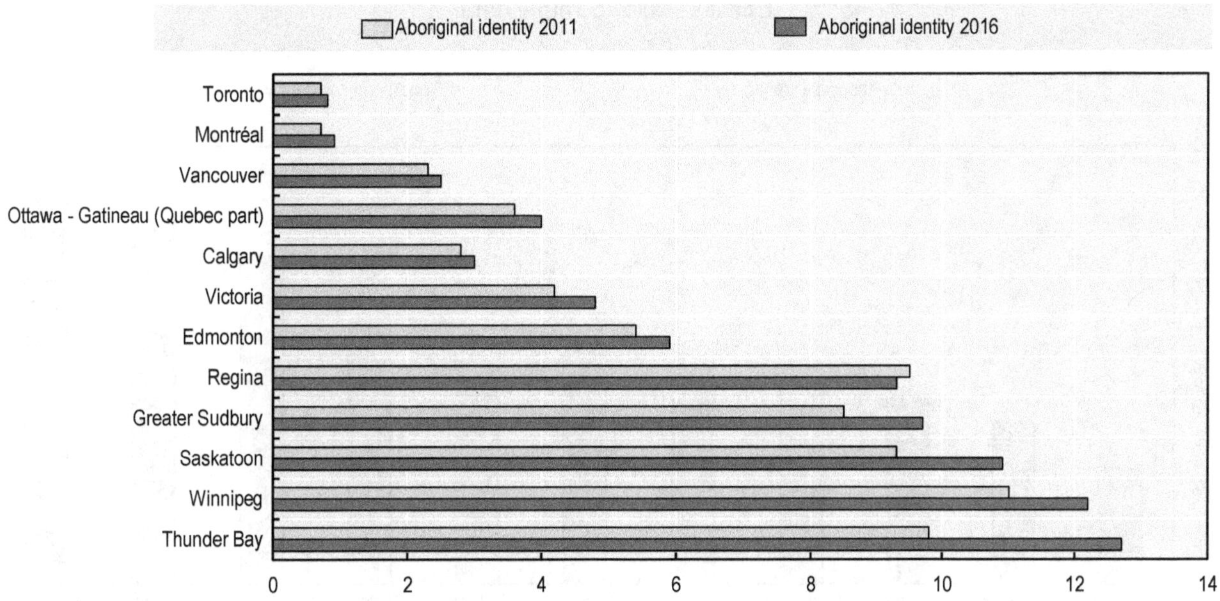

Aboriginal identity 2011 | Aboriginal identity 2016

Toronto
Montréal
Vancouver
Ottawa - Gatineau (Quebec part)
Calgary
Victoria
Edmonton
Regina
Greater Sudbury
Saskatoon
Winnipeg
Thunder Bay

0 2 4 6 8 10 12 14

Note: Only the 2016 counts provided in this table are unadjusted. Therefore, the 2016 Census counts are not based on adjusted counts for the incompletely enumerated Indian reserves and Indian settlements of previous census years, while the percentage change is based on adjusted counts.

Source: Statistics Canada (2016), 2016 Census of Population. Aboriginal identity population by both sexes, total - age, 2016 % distribution, Canada and census metropolitan areas and census agglomerations, 2016 Census – 25% Sample data, Statistics Canada Catalogue no. 98-402-X2016009. Ottawa. Released 25 October 2017, http://www12.statcan.gc.ca/census-recensement/2016/dp-pd/hlt-fst/abo-aut/Table.cfm?Lang=Eng&T=102&D1=4&D2=1&D3=1&RPP=50&PR=0&SR=1&S=84&O=D.

StatLink http://dx.doi.org/10.1787/888933724328

Over the last ten years, the urban Indigenous population in Canada has been growing steadily. Figure 4.5 illustrates that during the last decade, many of Canada's major cities have seen significant growth in the overall proportion of the city population reporting Indigenous identity versus non-Indigenous People (Statistics Canada, 2017b). This rapid rate of growth can be attributed to a number of common demographic factors, such as: fertility, mobility and migration. Another important factor is the increasing tendency for people to identify themselves as Indigenous, who may not have done so in previous censuses.

Figure 4.5. Aboriginal identity population by both sexes, total - age, % change (2006 to 2016), Canada and census metropolitan areas and census agglomerations, 2016 Census – 25% Sample data

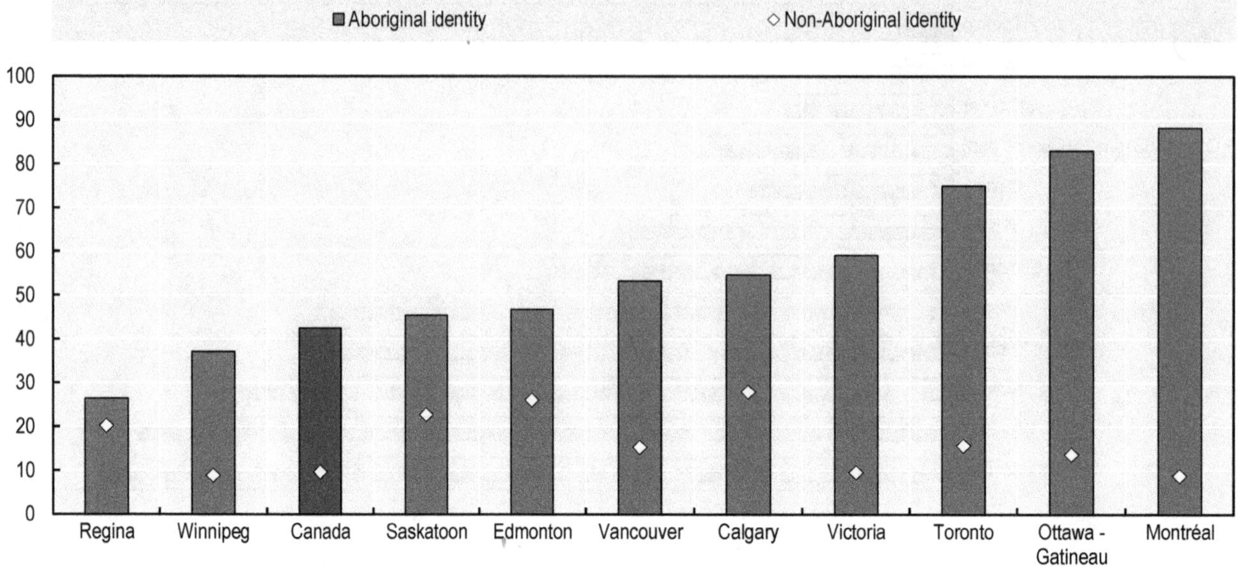

Note: Only the 2016 counts provided in this table are unadjusted. The growth rates for the Aboriginal identity population for the periods 2011 to 2016 and 2006 to 2016 have been adjusted for incompletely enumerated Indian reserves and Indian settlements, and other changes in reserves to allow for comparison of the different census year periods.

Source: Statistics Canada (2016), 2016 Census of Population. Aboriginal identity population by both sexes, total - age, % change (2006 to 2016), Canada and census metropolitan areas and census agglomerations, 2016 Census – 25% Sample data, Statistics Canada Catalogue no. 98-402-X2016009. Ottawa. Released 25 October 2017, http://www12.statcan.gc.ca/census-recensement/2016/dp-pd/hlt-fst/abo aut/Table.cfm?Lang=Eng&T=102&S=84&O=D&RPP=9999.

StatLink http://dx.doi.org/10.1787/888933724347

Understanding the socio-economic outcomes of Canada's urban Indigenous population

When comparing the percentage of the population not in the labour force, one can see large gaps between the Indigenous and non-Indigenous population across Canada's largest cities. The gap was particularly high in Winnipeg, Quebec City, Thunder Bay, and Edmonton.

While Indigenous socio-economic outcomes often trail the non-Indigenous population, Statistics Canada notes that Canada's urban Indigenous population is also very mobile. One in four urban Indigenous People were living in a different residence one year prior to the 2006 Census, by moving within the same city or moving from a different community, like a First Nation Reserve or another urban or rural area (Statistics Canada, 2010). This high rate of mobility creates some challenges for accessing and providing services, particularly services like education, employment training and housing.

Figure 4.6. Percentage of Indigenous and non-Indigenous identity populations not in the labour force, ages 15-64, most-populated Canadian metropolitan areas, 2016

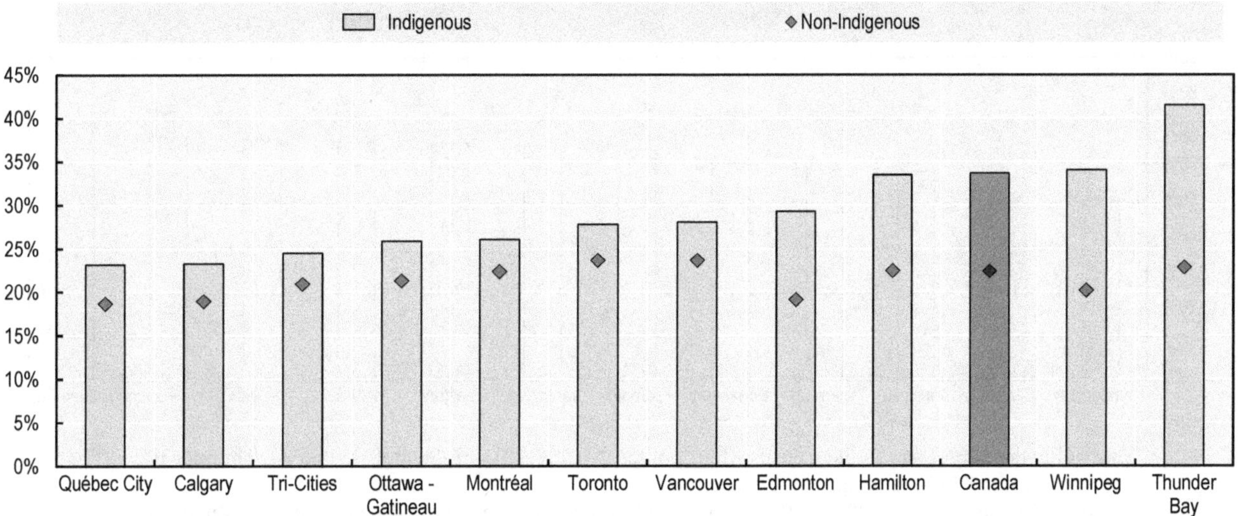

Note: Thunder Bay refers to the Census Metropolitan Area (CMA) of Greater Sudbury – Thunder Bay. Tri-Cities stands for Kitchener-Cambridge-Waterloo CMA.

Source: Statistics Canada (2016), 2016 Census of Population. Canada and census metropolitan areas and census agglomerations, 2016 Census – 25% Sample data, data extracted by Employment and Skills Development Canada, received 11 April 2018.

StatLink http://dx.doi.org/10.1787/888933724366

Figure 4.7 shows the employment rate gap between Indigenous and non-Indigenous groups across Canada's largest cities. On this indicator, there are fairly significant gaps, especially in places such as Thunder Bay (22.1%), Winnipeg (17.1%), Edmonton (13.9%), and Hamilton (13.8%). In contrast, Ottawa-Gatineau (5.5%) and Montréal (5.6%) have the lowest gaps in employment rates between the outcomes of the Indigenous and non-Indigenous population (Statistics Canada, 2016b).

Substantial differences can also be seen within the unemployment rate (see Figure 4.8) between the Indigenous and non-Indigenous population. In Ottawa-Gatineau, Québec City and Montréal, there is at least a 3 percentage point difference between the two groups. While Montreal was the highest performer in 2016, with very similar outcomes between Indigenous and non-Indigenous groups at one of the lowest unemployment rates within Canadian CMAs, Ottawa-Gatineau and Québec City have also improved their outcomes over the past five years (Statistics Canada, 2011; Statistics Canada, 2016b).

Figure 4.7. Employment rates of Indigenous and non-Indigenous identity populations, ages 15-64, most-populated Canadian metropolitan areas, 2016

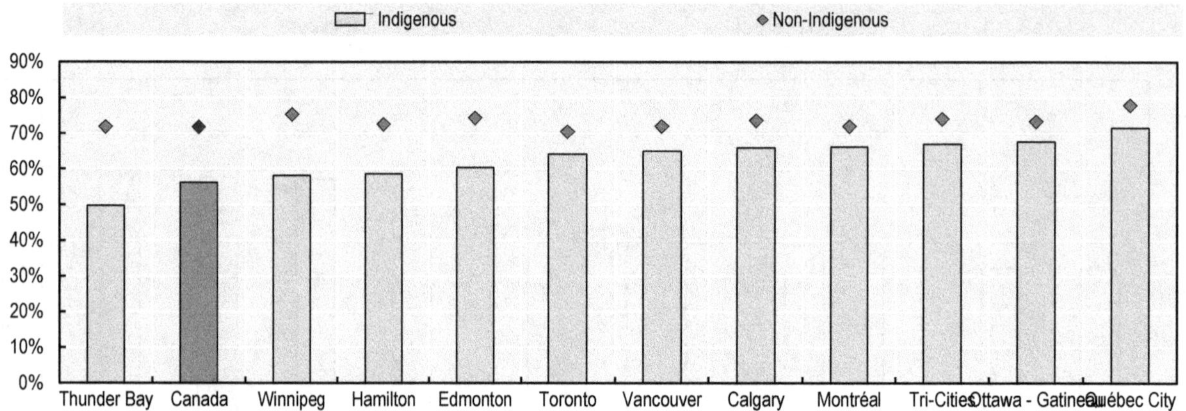

Note: Thunder Bay refers to the Census Metropolitan Area (CMA) of Greater Sudbury – Thunder Bay. Tri-Cities stands for Kitchener-Cambridge-Waterloo CMA.

Source: Statistics Canada (2016), 2016 Census of Population. Canada and census metropolitan areas and census agglomerations, 2016 Census – 25% Sample data, data extracted by Employment and Skills Development Canada, received 11 April 2018.

StatLink http://dx.doi.org/10.1787/888933724385

Figure 4.8. Unemployment rates of Indigenous and non-Indigenous identity populations, ages 15-64, most-populated Canadian metropolitan areas, %, 2016

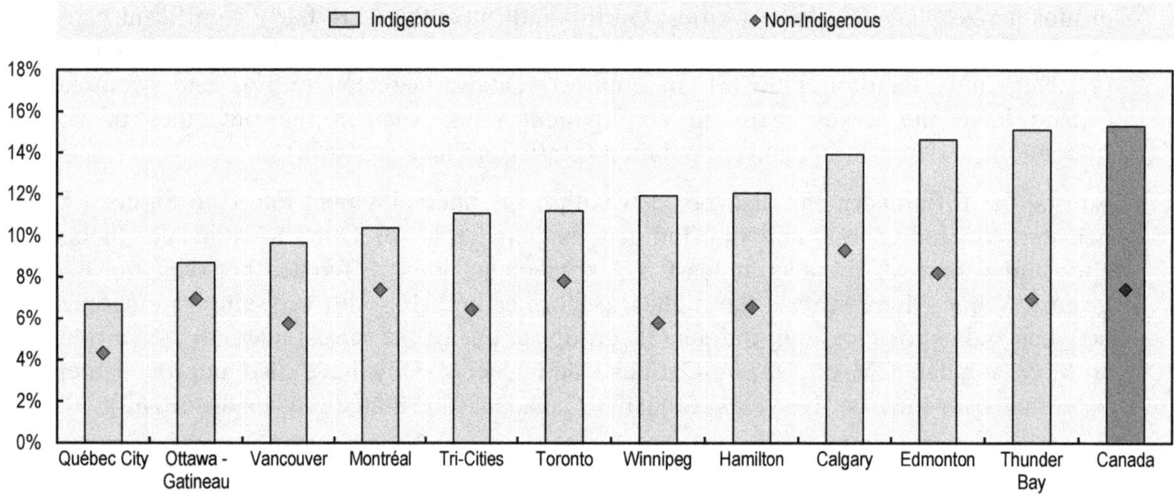

Note: Thunder Bay refers to the Census Metropolitan Area (CMA) of Greater Sudbury – Thunder Bay. Tri-Cities stands for Kitchener-Cambridge-Waterloo CMA.

Source: Statistics Canada (2016), 2016 Census of Population. Canada and census metropolitan areas and census agglomerations, 2016 Census – 25% Sample data, data extracted by Employment and Skills Development Canada, received 11 April 2018.

StatLink http://dx.doi.org/10.1787/888933724404

Urban Indigenous policies and programmes in Canada

Urban Programming

Delivered by Indigenous and Northern Affairs Canada, Urban Programming for Indigenous People, which replaces the former Urban Aboriginal Strategy, is designed to assist First Nations (status and non-status), Inuit and Métis People living in or transitioning to urban centres. The programming has four streams of funding including organisational capacity, programmes and services, coalitions and research and innovation. Through targeted programme support for youth, women, vulnerable populations, transition services, outreach, and community wellbeing, the Urban Programming for Indigenous People will directly contribute to the improvement of the socio-economic opportunities for urban Indigenous Canadians. Funding for this programme is CAD 43 million annually over five years (2017-2022).

The national Indigenous stakeholders involved in the implementation of programmes are the Métis Nation, the Inuit Tapiriit Kanatami and the friendship centre movement. This programme has a specific funding stream to support Local Coalitions. These Coalitions will bring together all orders of government, local organisations, and other stakeholders to identify local needs and priorities and ensure efficient and coordinated delivery of urban Indigenous programmes. The primary goals are to promote collaboration at the local level, identify local needs and develop local plans on how to best address and prioritize needs. The Coalitions need to demonstrate inclusiveness and encourage the active participation of a wide range of stakeholders. Non-Indigenous stakeholders include the Federation of Canadian Municipalities and provincial and municipal governments. Other federal departments/agencies providing complementary programmes and services for urban Indigenous People are also involved in the implementation of new programming.

In the summer and fall of 2016, INAC conducted a multifaceted engagement regarding the needs of the urban Indigenous community, and how these needs could be addressed through renewed urban programming. Engagement included the following activities: twenty-one roundtables across Canada, town hall meetings hosted by parliamentarians, specific engagement activities organized by National Indigenous Organizations targeting their respective members. Specific sessions were also held with the Métis Nation through the Métis National Council, Tungasuvvingat Inuit, the Metro Vancouver Aboriginal Executive Council and the Toronto Aboriginal Support Services.

Outreach efforts

In keeping with the Canadian Government's approach to ensure inclusive growth, ESDC and Service Canada have undertaken important outreach efforts, to further identify and address barriers that may impact access to the benefits by these more vulnerable communities. Specifically, outreach by Service Canada is focused on:

- Establishing or strengthening relationships with Reserve and Northern communities;
- Understanding barriers to uptake and the extent in each community, and
- Tailoring outreach support in a manner respectful of the communities and increase the likelihood of increasing uptake.

Initial efforts confirmed a potential challenge with benefit uptake on reserves, and further outreach was undertaken to help define it. To help accomplish this, Service Canada and the Canadian Revenue Agency (CRA) have been engaging with Reserve and Northern communities across the country to raise awareness of the Canada Child Benefit (CCB). Efforts include information sessions on the CCB, and other benefits, and how to access. Social Insurance Number (SIN) services on reserves have also been provided.

Moving forward, Service Canada and the CRA will continue to visit Reserves and Northern communities to support tax filing and the benefits application process. As more analysis of uptake becomes available, ESDC will continue to refine the outreach approach to maximize the effectiveness of this activity.

Indigenous initiatives managed at the city level – lessons from the case studies

The City of Winnipeg

Winnipeg has the largest Indigenous population of any city in Canada with 92 810 people identifying as Indigenous — First Nations, Métis and Inuit. Looking across Canada, the Métis population (587 545) had the largest increase of any of the groups between 2006 and 2016, rising 51.2%. The largest population is in Winnipeg, which had 52 130 Métis in 2016, an increase of 28%. Given the significant number of Indigenous People within the city, a number of initiatives have been launched to improve labour market and economic development outcomes while also supporting the reconciliation process.

For example, in July 2010, the City of Winnipeg partnered with the Province of Manitoba as well as the Canadian federal government to sign a memorandum of collaboration to work together to better align resources to improve the socio-economic outcomes of Indigenous People in Winnipeg. An Intergovernmental Strategic Indigenous Alignment (ISIA) Working Group was established to develop a five year strategic plan. The working group included: City of Winnipeg, Manager of Indigenous Relations; Manitoba Indigenous and Municipal Relations, Director of Policy and Strategic Initiatives; and Indigenous and Northern Affairs Canada, Manitoba Regional Director.

The three levels of government identified four strategic areas of intergovernmental collaboration: 1) Education, Training, and Lifelong Learning; 2) Employment and Economic Development; 3) Building Capacity, Community Supports and Personal Engagement; and Supporting Community Wellness and Safety. The initial memorandum of collaboration also identified nine principles, which would guide how the three levels of government would work together.

An evaluation on this multi-governance collaboration was carried out in 2015 by the City of Winnipeg. It found that there are multiple options for intergovernmental alignment: however alignment is only a means to an end, and deep alignment is difficult to achieve. The evaluation noted that the volume, pace and quality of ISIA work was limited by side-of-the-desk participation, membership turnover, and insufficient resources for coordination support. One of the key recommendations from this evaluation was the need to establish a dedicated coordination support unit and consider a shared pool of funding to develop joint projects and programmes.

Going forward, in 2015 the ISIA Working Group has developed an Administrative Letter of Understanding with a supporting Statement of Work which outlines four priority areas, strategies and activities the group will collaborate on and have defined:

- **Welcoming Winnipeg**: to create a welcoming environment in the City of Winnipeg, increase cultural awareness through highlighting Indigenous People's roles and contributions in the evolution of the City of Winnipeg and engaging newcomers and visitors to build on lasting relationships for our shared future;

- **Urban Reserves**: to support Indigenous Communities to develop Urban Reserves or Urban Economic Development Zones within the City of Winnipeg and to support the City of Winnipeg in its efforts to negotiate Municipal Development Service Agreements (MDSAs) with various First Nations, and
- **Sustainable Livelihoods Model project**: to update a current database of services accessed by Winnipeg's Indigenous population, the project will examine and layer on demographic information to try to determine if the existing programmes and services match where the Indigenous population of Winnipeg may be at. This information will increase knowledge about community programmes and services for individuals, community organisations, and funders.

Local leadership in Winnipeg has been critical in building a sense of community awareness and aligning efforts to improve Indigenous outcomes. Recently, the Mayor of Winnipeg established the Mayor's Indigenous Advisory Circle (MIAC) which is a promising example of partnership working that could be emulated in other cities in Canada (see Box 4.2).

Box 4.2. City of Winnipeg – Mayor's Indigenous Advisory Council

In 2015, the Mayor of the City of Winnipeg announced the establishment of a Mayor's Indigenous Advisory Circle (MIAC). The role of the MIAC is to advise on policies the City of Winnipeg can implement to continue to build awareness, bridges and understanding between the Indigenous and non-Indigenous community. Meetings of the Advisory Circle are held quarterly and members include Indigenous elders, First Nation Chiefs, as well as members from the education and university sectors, and Aboriginal Chamber of Commerce.

A key achievement of the MIAC is the Indigenous Accord, which was adopted by City Council on March 22, 2017. The Indigenous Accord is living document to guide the shared commitment to the Journey of Reconciliation in Winnipeg. Winnipeg's Indigenous Accord is not a single-time event, but an ongoing responsibility accepted by signatories, who through becoming partners to the Accord agree to report the success of their commitment to reconciliation. It outlines a vision of reconciliation as well as a series of important commitments and principles.

Source: City of Winnipeg (2018), Winnipeg's Indigenous Accord, available at: http://www.winnipeg.ca/Indigenous/WIA/default.stm.

The City of Calgary

The City of Calgary is situated in the traditional territory of the Niitsitapi and the people of Treaty 7 at the confluence of the Elbow River and the Bow River. Calgary Indigenous population comprises 17 955 First Nations, 22 220 Métis, and 440 Inuit.

The Calgary Aboriginal Urban Affairs Committee (CAUAC) has been established as a collaborative effort between The City of Calgary and Indigenous communities to address and resolve issues pertaining to urban Indigenous residents. On behalf of City Council, the CAUAC investigates areas of concern to people of Aboriginal ancestry and makes recommendations on policies and resolutions that give urban Indigenous People a more meaningful role within the Calgary community.

After consultations with Treaty 7 traditional knowledge keepers, urban Indigenous People and City stakeholders, the CAUAC proposed the Indigenous Policy and Indigenous Policy Framework. Together, they recommend and guide meaningful long-term efforts to bring Indigenous identities, histories, cultures, languages, traditions, principles, world views, relationships and ways of knowing into municipal planning, advising and decision-making efforts. City Council approved the policy and framework in April 2017.

The purpose of this Council Policy is guide the city council on how best to listen to, learn from, and act on ways forward with Indigenous communities in planning, advising and decision-making. The City's Indigenous Policy Framework consists of four ways forward that include: 1) Ways of Knowing; 2) Ways of Engaging; 3) Ways of Building Relationships; and 4) Ways Towards Equitable Environments. There are several proposed policy statements, emerging from the Policy Framework (see Box 6.3 for a summary).

In 2017, City Council adopted the Indigenous Policy Framework to help guide the City's efforts to be responsive to the needs of Indigenous People in Calgary (see Box 4.3).

Consultations and partnerships with Indigenous People is also a central piece of the 10 year Economic Strategy of Calgary, which was last updated in 2014. The Strategy was developed through a deep stakeholder consultation process, led by the Mayor of Calgary with key organisations having been requested to serve on the Leadership and Implementation Committee which meets three times annually to discuss progress. The 10 year Economic Strategy outlines 31 actions of which a key component is assisting First Nations and Indigenous People to build their professional networks. The strategy also highlights the importance of developing entrepreneurial programmes specific to First Nations and Indigenous youth.

The city also plays a key role as a service contact point for many First Nations and Indigenous People, often coordinating and connecting these individuals to services offered by organisations in the city such as Community Futures Treaty Seven, Aboriginal Futures Career and Training Centre, as well as Métis Nation of Alberta Employment Services Zone III.

One interesting programme is the Indigenous Awareness E-learning programme which is targeted to employers and designed to help an employer or supervisor of Indigenous employees understand the current social, economic, and political situation of Indigenous People and provide tools to increase Indigenous employment and retention. This E-learning course can be taken at any time and modules taken in any order.

Box 4.3. Indigenous Policy Framework for the City of Calgary

The City of Calgary has established an Indigenous Policy Framework, which outlines the following actions along four pillars:

Ways of Knowing

- The City of Calgary should undertake formal cross-cultural awareness and education on Indigenous histories, cultures, languages, worldviews, Indigenous and treaty rights, Treaty 7, and relationships, as professional development for City staff and Council and part of broader awareness for Calgarians where appropriate.
- The City of Calgary should support learning opportunities for City Administration to share and exchange knowledge with Treaty 7 First Nations on matters of historical, traditional, and cultural significance due to their traditional territory and urban Indigenous People on matters of contemporary significance.

Ways of Engaging

- The City of Calgary will support and advance multiple projects to respectfully engage Treaty 7 First Nations Knowledge Keepers by identifying opportunities early in the planning of City projects, processes and events related to matters of historical, traditional, and cultural significance to Treaty 7 First Nations.
- The City of Calgary will develop engagement processes and opportunities with Treaty 7 First Nations on matters of historical, traditional, and cultural significance due to their traditional territory.
- The City of Calgary will develop engagement processes and opportunities with Indigenous communities, leadership, and organisations on matters of contemporary significance.

Ways of Building Relationships

- The City of Calgary will prioritize, form and maintain beneficial leadership-to-leadership relationships with Treaty 7 First Nations and urban Indigenous communities based on mutual recognition, mutual respect, and shared responsibility.
- The City of Calgary shall work together with Treaty 7 First Nations to:
  - Strengthen understandings of the diverse identities, histories, cultures, languages, worldviews, relationships, and connections to the land of individual Treaty 7 First Nations;
  - Identify matters of common interest and understand community priorities;
  - Improve communication through dialogue and formal agreements;
  - Explore opportunities to collaborate on joint initiatives, policies, strategies, and decision making processes;
  - Explore opportunities for The City to reflect on the shared foundations and history of the traditional territory through communication, ceremony, practices and capacity-building, and
  - Find common ground from which to reconcile matters of historical, cultural, and traditional significance, including territorial matters with Treaty 7 leadership.
- The City of Calgary will work together with urban Indigenous People, community leaders and organisations when related to corporate matters to:
- Strengthen understandings of the diverse identities, histories, languages, cultures

perspectives, and lived experiences of First Nations, Métis and Inuit People who call Calgary home or have an historical association with the land within the boundaries of Calgary;
- o Identify matters of common interest and understand community opportunities;
- o Improve communication through dialogue and formal agreements;
- o Explore opportunities to collaborate on joint initiatives, policies, strategies, and decision-making processes;
- o Explore opportunities for The City to reflect on the shared foundations and history of the traditional territory as it relates to urban Indigenous communities through communication, ceremony, practices, and capacity-building and
- o Find common ground from which to reconcile matters of contemporary significance.

Ways Towards Equitable Environments

- The City of Calgary, when updating existing policies and/or practices, will strive to understand the potential impacts on Treaty 7 First Nations and other Indigenous communities.
- The City of Calgary will explore opportunities for Administration to collaborate with Indigenous communities to produce inclusive and equitable amendments to include Indigenous practices.

The City of Calgary, when developing new policies and/or practices, will explore opportunities to collaborate on meaningful and innovative strategic directions and approaches with Treaty 7 First Nations and other appropriate Indigenous communities.

Thunder Bay, Ontario

Ontario is Canada's second largest and most populous province, covering approximately 1 million square kilometres. In 2017, Ontario's population increased by 1.6% to a total of 14 193 384 people (Statistics Canada, 2017a). The 2016 census counted 1.67 million Indigenous People in Canada accounting for approximately 4.9% of the total population. As of 2016, a total of 179 970 Indigenous People resided in Ontario, representing 1.34% of the provincial population.

With a population of 124 200, Thunder Bay is the largest city in North-western Ontario and is home to nearly half of the region's population. It is located on the north shore of Lake Superior and is often referred to as the Lakehead because it is situated at the head of the Great Lakes. In 2016, 12.7% (15 445) of the population of Thunder Bay had an Indigenous identity (Statistics Canada, 2017a). In the latest available Canadian Census, among all CMAs in the country, Thunder Bay's Indigenous People accounted for the highest proportion (12.7%) of the overall population.

In Thunder Bay, an Aboriginal Liaison Strategy has been established by the City Council. The Aboriginal Liaison plays a lead role in establishing relationships within the City's growing urban Indigenous community as well as with those organisations, agencies and groups representing and serving the Indigenous community within the City. The City aims to strengthen understanding between the Indigenous community and the City. This process of engagement will lead to the identification and agreement of urban Indigenous priorities within Thunder Bay. In addition, the Aboriginal Liaison will work within the

City to raise awareness and understanding of the cultural protocols and sensitivities involved in engaging with and serving the Indigenous community.

The plan will be reviewed each year, to identify the areas of focus for the next working year and the financial supports that will be required. Indicators of success have been identified as:

- Improvements to Statistics Canada numbers (Employment, education, homelessness, poverty);
- Increased participation by the Indigenous community in City services and programmes;
- Indigenous People becoming more engaged in municipal politics and governance (boards and committees);
- Feeling welcomed and respected;
- More and on-going involvement with Mayor, Council and Administration and
- Seeing Indigenous People being positively represented in the community.

Interestingly, one of the strategies outlined in Thunder Bay's Aboriginal Liaison Strategy includes focus on the City's role as an employer of Indigenous People. The Strategy notes the City of Thunder Bay should become an employer of choice for Indigenous People. This includes developing culturally sensitive and specific recruitment materials to market working at the City to Indigenous communities as well internship programmes to provide work experience opportunities. The City also outlines the importance of cultural sensitivity training to all new employees as part of their orientation.

Fredericton, New Brunswick

Fredericton is the capital of New Brunswick. The city is nestled in the west-central portion of the province, along the shores of the Saint John River, which stands to be the prevailing natural feature of the area. Being one of the main urban centres in New Brunswick, the city had a population of 101 760 in the 2016 census. In 2016, 15% of Indigenous People in New Brunswick lived in Fredericton. Of those, 76% identified as First Nations (Statistics Canada, 2017a).

In 2017, the City of Fredericton announced a Transit Fare Assistance Program, which provides regular single-ride and Para Transit tickets to 36 community agencies or programmes – many of whom work with Indigenous People and clients. The programme is designed to provide additional support to community groups as they assist their clients' efforts to attend medical appointments, access education and training, seek employment or visit service providers.

In the area of economic development, the City of Fredericton works with Ignite Fredericton, which is the region's business focused economic development corporation offering assistance to business to start, grow, and locate in Fredericton. Ignite Fredericton offers a range of business advice services and would assist in connecting Indigenous People to customised supports. The City of Fredericton does not have an overall Indigenous policy framework, which can be found in the other cities examined at part of this OECD study. This is likely because of its smaller size and capacity relative to Calgary, Winnipeg, and Thunder Bay.

Critical success factors identified from the case studies

Policy coordination among federal, provincial, and local governments

Under *the Indian Act*, the federal government has traditionally defined its responsibility to Indigenous People as focused only those persons living on-reserves. Furthermore, provinces and cities in Canada have tended to see all Indigenous People (even those in cities) as a federal responsibility (Carli, 2013).

While the examples from Winnipeg, Calgary, and Thunder Bay show strategic efforts to align programmes and services to meet the needs of urban Indigenous People, policy coordination and partnership working with Indigenous communities across levels of government remains an on-going challenge. Some researchers have suggested that federal, provincial, and municipal governments rarely agree upon financial responsibility for Indigenous People in an urban setting, often resulting in a "policy patchwork" with jurisdictional ambiguities (Marcie Snyder, 2015). Frequently, Indigenous People experience difficulty in obtaining service information and are not aware of what services are available – both in situations where an Indigenous person may be moving from an on-reserve setting to a city or even when an Indigenous person may be moving within a city.

At the local municipal level in Canada, there is a broad mix of federal, provincial, and municipal programming which aims to improve the outcomes of Indigenous People, who are often face multiple barriers to employment. In some cases, Indigenous service delivery can often overlap and create duplication with several organisations operating in the same policy space. Other researchers have observed instances of infrequent communication reducing key partners' impact at the local level (Alcantara & Nelles, 2016). Increased frequency and quality of communication between service providers can be a critical success factor in producing successful outcomes within partnerships.

Good governance is important to make decisions that are informed, open and transparent. By collectively conversing with local stakeholders, organisations can make assessments that reflect the broad interest of the community and in turn promote community confidence.

Across the case studies examined for this OECD study, all are interested in constantly engaging with key stakeholders to discuss workforce gaps and arising opportunities. It was noted by many of the case study representatives that by having an open dialogue, all parties are aware of communities' vision for the future and can better align programmes and services to meet Indigenous People's needs and local opportunities.

Coordinating access to services for urban Indigenous People

A clear theme that emerged from the case study analysis of this OECD study is the need to better coordinate access to services for urban Indigenous People. Many urban Indigenous People often find it difficult to know where and how to access programmes and services, which can further exacerbate their disadvantage. Furthermore, often times, many service delivery organisations operating within cities across Canada would not necessary provide culturally sensitive services to Indigenous People. This situation can be especially challenging for Indigenous People who are moving from an on-reserve setting into an urban area. There is a need to coordinate services at the municipal level to ensure that clearer information is provided to indigenous person on where to go to access employment, skills development, and other training services.

Local leadership

There is a clear and important role to be played at the city level by Mayors, who bring together local service delivery organisations alongside the federal and provincial governments to align funding and policy objectives. Mayors regularly participate in local meetings with Indigenous communities to hear about their challenges and identify opportunities to labour market success. The examples from Winnipeg, Thunder Bay, and Calgary show a clear leadership role being taken by the municipal government to raise awareness of the importance of providing specific and customised supports to Indigenous People. These cities are also demonstrating leadership by articulating strategic policy frameworks targeted to the urban Indigenous population which is fundamental for better coordinating services and designing policy interventions.

Developing social capital and community-driven initiatives

In addition to enhanced policy coordination, a sense of community capital can further enhance local co-operation. In the literature, this has been defined as communities having a shared civic identity (Alcantara & Nelles, 2016). Many local initiatives can gain momentum because the communities (e.g. Indigenous and non-Indigenous People) identify and empathise with each other. Often, the most significant improvements in lives of Indigenous People come from within the community itself. While some initiatives have been small in scale, their impact is substantial. Many of these programmes also have the potential to be scalable depending on the local context in which they were and implemented and if the community desires.

These initiatives for Indigenous People should be led by Indigenous People, seeking to understand the needs of the population while simultaneously giving the Indigenous People their own autonomy and resources to achieve their goals. Approaches that disproportionately focus on the deficiencies of Indigenous communities are inaccurate and unhelpful. Therefore, any policy or programme that seeks to ameliorate the outcomes of Indigenous People needs to ascertain and centralise how Indigenous People wish to define success in the given context.

References

Alcantara, C. and J. Nelles (2016), *Indigenous communities and local governments are powerful partners*, http://policyoptions.irpp.org/magazines/august-2016/indigenous-communities-and-local-governments-are-powerful-partners/ (accessed on 28 August 2017).

Carli, V. (2013), *The City as a "space of opportunity": Urban Indigenous Experiences and Community Safety Partnerships*, Thompson Education Publishing.

City of Winnipeg (2018), Winnipeg's Indigenous Accord, available at http://www.winnipeg.ca/Indigenous/WIA/default.stm.

Indigeneous and Northern Affairs Canada (2018), *Urban Indigeneous Peoples*, https://www.aadnc-aandc.gc.ca/eng/1100100014265/1369225120949.

Marcie Snyder, K. (2015), "Examining the Urban Aboriginal Policy Gap: Impacts on Service Delivery for Mobile Aboriginal Peoples in Winnipeg, Canada", *Aboriginal Policy Studies*, pp. 3-27.

OECD (2017), *National Urban Policy in OECD Countries*, OECD Publishing, Paris, http://dx.doi.org/10.1787/9789264271906-en.

OECD (2018), "Subnational government structure and finance", OECD Regional Statistics (database).

Ontario Ministry of Municipal Affairs (2018), available at http://www.mah.gov.on.ca/Page343.aspx.

Statistics Canada (2010), *Urban Aboriginal population in Canada*, Statistics Canada.

Statistics Canada (2011), *Calculations based on Public Use Microdata File*, http://www12.statcan.gc.ca/nhs-enm/2011/dp-pd/pumf-fmgd/index-eng.cfm.

Statistics Canada (2016), 2016 Census of Population. Aboriginal identity population by both sexes, total - age, 2016 counts, Canada and census metropolitan areas and census agglomerations, 2016 Census – 25% Sample data, Statistics Canada Catalogue no. 98-402-X2016009. Ottawa. Released 25 October 2017, http://www12.statcan.gc.ca/census-recensement/2016/dp-pd/hlt-fst/abo-aut/Table.cfm?Lang=Eng&T=102&S=102&O=D&RPP=9999.

Statistics Canada (2016), 2016 Census of Population. Canada and census metropolitan areas and census agglomerations, 2016 Census – 25% Sample data, data extracted by Employment and Skills Development Canada, received 11 April 2018.

Statistics Canada (2017a), *Aboriginal peoples in Canada: Key results from the 2016 Census*, http://www.statcan.gc.ca/daily-quotidien/171025/dq171025a-eng.htm.

Statistics Canada (2017b), *Aboriginal Peoples Highlight Tables, 2016 Census*, NHS 2016, http://www12.statcan.gc.ca/census-recensement/2016/dp-pd/hlt-fst/abo-aut/Table.cfm?Lang=Eng&T=102&S=84&O=D&RPP=9999 (accessed on 14 November 2017).

Statistics Canada (2017), 2016 Census of Population. Aboriginal identity population by both sexes, total - age, 2016 counts, Canada and census metropolitan areas and census agglomerations, 2016 Census – 25% Sample data, Statistics Canada Catalogue no. 98-402-X2016009. Ottawa. Released 25 October 2017, http://www12.statcan.gc.ca/census-recensement/2016/dp-pd/hlt-fst/abo-aut/Table.cfm?Lang=Eng&T=102&S=102&O=D&RPP=9999.

Chapter 5. Recommendations

Ensuring that Indigenous People have equal opportunity to participate in the labour market is fundamental to promote inclusive growth in Canada. This requires robust active labour market, skills, and economic development programmes to foster local partnerships and provide culturally sensitive services. Indigenous communities should be given every opportunity to take leadership in managing and delivering policies and programmes. This chapter outlines key recommendations emerging from this OECD study on Indigenous People in Canada.

Recommendations emerging from this OECD study

This OECD study has identified a number of opportunities and challenges facing Indigenous People in Canada. To work towards reconciliation as well as meeting commitments under the United Nations Declaration on the Rights of Indigenous Peoples, it is clear that well designed labour market and skills policies have a fundamental role to play in addressing the barriers to employment faced by Indigenous People, while also respecting the principle of advancing self-determination.

The Indigenous population is a growing source of labour supply within Canada. There are both economic and social reasons to ensure that Indigenous People are given every opportunity to succeed within the labour market and broader Canadian economy. This report has shown that while there are gaps between the Indigenous and non-Indigenous population, significant improvements and efforts are also being made at both the federal and local level.

The following recommendations and policy insights emerge from the data and in-depth case study analysis on Indigenous employment and skills policies in Canada.

Consider injecting additional flexibility into the management of Indigenous labour market and skills training programming

Indigenous labour market programming is principally delivered through the Indigenous Skills and Employment Strategy (ISETS) as well as the Skills and Partnerships Fund (SPF). The analysis of four case studies conducted as part of this study highlights a number of key strengths and innovations happening at the local level. In all case studies, it is clear that there are experienced staff that are committed to working in partnership with Indigenous communities to provide employment and skills training that leads to a good job. In Winnipeg, Manitoba, the Centre for Aboriginal Human Resource Development is a particularly strong example of a one-stop centre providing the full range of "cradle to grave" services from child care, employment counselling and placement, skills development, housing, as well as career coaching and mentoring.

Going forward, there are benefits to be achieved from examining how to inject additional flexibility into the management of Indigenous labour market programming. This could be achieved by exploring the potential for integrating funding across programmes as well as easing the reporting and accountability requirements on Indigenous agreement holders. Recently announced program changes, including establishment of 10 year agreements with the renewal of ASETs into ISETs will provide opportunities for service providers to undertake long-term strategic planning. It is important that policies work in partnership with Indigenous communities as opposed to administering a programme to a community. Additional flexibility for service delivery and labour market programming would likely provide incentives to work in partnership with employers and training institutions.

In the area of skills training, flexibility could be considered in terms of whether Indigenous service providers can be given more latitude to fund postsecondary education and training. Indigenous People often need more financial and social support to participate in this type of training and there seems to be uncertainty regarding whether this type of activity is eligible for funding. In some cases, rigidity within the vocational education and training system which is generally managed by provinces and territories in Canada can restrict the ability of Indigenous organizations to offer more specific and customised skills training programmes for Indigenous learners.

It is important to note that actions are already being taken in this area. For example, through the SPF, service delivery organisations implementing training to employment projects are required to establish partnerships with employers to achieve their objectives. Since the development of these partnerships can fluctuate based on industry priorities and/or economic factors, the government provided implementing organisations with flexibility to establish arrangements with new partners if the original employer withdraws from the project due to unforeseen circumstances.

Furthermore, the Federal Government's recent Budget 2018 announced a number of changes to Indigenous labour market programming, including establishing ten year agreements. This is a welcome development. The ISET programme places a stronger focus on training for high quality and better paying jobs, which is a welcome development. Furthermore, the programme also aims to provide more flexibility to Indigenous agreement holder in the management of employment programmes, which will enable greater leadership at the local level in the delivery of services.

Continue work to improve alignment of federal and provincial Indigenous labour market programming

Indigenous labour market and skills programming at the local level could benefit from stronger coordination across federal departments as well as between federal and provincial levels of government in Canada. Other federal departments as well as provincial level ministries are involved in Indigenous programming (and urban programming). With the quick roll out of four new programming streams of the federal Urban Programming for Indigenous People in a short implementation window, there is a risk of programme and service delivery duplication. Collaborative work between federal, provincial, and territorial governments and Indigenous organizations to identify and maximize program complementarity will be key. It should also be noted that multiple programme streams may also be more effective to providing outreach to Indigenous People who often face multiple barriers to employment. There is an opportunity to further leverage the existing inter-governmental forums such as the FLMM and LMMCs to better engage Indigenous organisations and identify stronger linkages between federal, provincial, and indigenous labour market programming at the local level.

Some Indigenous service delivery organisations are operating on a funding model based on a mix of federal and provincial programmes each with their own accountability requirements. Going forward, there could be a benefit to explore how to combine these funding envelopes into one single programme envelope based on a streamlined outcomes-based delivery model which enable Indigenous communities to assume more leadership on implementation locally.

It will be critical that other labour market programmes (e.g. the Labour Market Development Agreements and the Workforce Development Agreement, the federal Youth Employment Strategy, and Indigenous and Northern Affairs Canada programming) be well aligned with Employment and Social Development Canada's Indigenous labour market programmes to ensure complementarity.

It should be highlighted that Employment and Social Development Canada is undertaking action in this area. For example, as part of the renewal of Indigenous labour market programmes, provincial and territorial governments were engaged to explore better policy linkages and alignment. In the 2016 Call for Proposal for the SPF, service delivery organisations were required to demonstrate a direct link to existing federal agreement holders. Furthermore, federal department working groups have been established to explore better linkages between Employment and Social Development Canada and Indigenous and Northern Affairs Canada. The federal government is also exploring how to better leverage existing intergovernmental fora on labour market issues to ensure greater programme complementarity, and to increase collaboration of these forums with Indigenous People to better respond to Indigenous needs.

Leverage the role of cities in addressing the needs of urban Indigenous People

Cities can be policy spaces of opportunity to test new ideas and pilot new ways of partnering with Indigenous organisations to design and deliver culturally-appropriate programmes and services to support Indigenous People living in urban areas. As highlighted in this report, traditionally, Indigenous People have been the constitutional domain of the federal government due to a number of legal obligations. It is important that both federal and provincial policies relating to urban Indigenous populations are designed in partnerships with cities to ensure that urban zones are safe, rewarding, and productive environments for Indigenous People. Given the role that municipal governments in Canada often play in delivering social assistance services, there may be an opportunity to be explored that enables cities to actively manage labour market and skills programming. It would be important that any move to provide cities with more autonomy in this policy space are accompanied by appropriate resources for them to be effective.

The recently announced new Urban Programming for Indigenous Peoples (UPIP) by the Canadian government is a welcome step to better target the urban indigenous population with an emphasis on projects that help Indigenous women transition out of shelters, support Indigenous People with addictions, as well as provide mentoring opportunities to Indigenous youth. Friendship Centres are helping many Indigenous People in urban centres across Canada access vital services. Following the examples highlighted in this report from Winnipeg and Thunder Bay, cities in Canada should seek opportunities to develop urban Indigenous strategies and specific Indigenous policy frameworks that aim to better link the range of Indigenous service providers and organisations and improve the labour market supports available to urban Indigenous People.

Improve the collection and use of Indigenous Labour Market Information (LMI)

Statistics Canada has observed a 19% increase in the Indigenous population between 2011 and 2016. Compared to the 4% growth rate of the non-Indigenous population during the same period, this enormous difference can both be accounted for by a higher fertility rate found within the Indigenous population compared to the non-Indigenous population and also the trend in more people declaring Indigenous status on the Census who have not previously done so. Current trends suggest this will continue in the future (Statistics Canada, 2018). These numbers are based on self-identification, which is different than Indian Status, which is determined under the federal *Indian Act*.

Variance in the overall number of Indigenous People is not the only issue related to data reliability. The difficulty in making conclusive findings regarding Indigenous outcomes is that data is often inconsistent and generalised. This is especially true regarding data at a local level in regards to Indigenous People.

Programme design and service delivery will be better informed by available, local, timely LMI. Findings from ESDC's 2015 evaluation of Indigenous labour market programmes identified that the lack of accurate and up to date local LMI constrained the ability of Indigenous communities to adequately support their annual operational planning, and the evaluation recommended strengthening agreement holders' access to timely LMI to support their service delivery. This issue was also raised by Indigenous partners during the engagement sessions of the Canadian government on the renewal of Indigenous labour market programming.

Improvements to Indigenous LMI could be greatly enhanced through collaborations with Indigenous groups at the local level. Indigenous groups could give insights as to how data collection could be strengthened to be more timely, reliable, consistent and relevant at a local level. In partnership with indigenous organisations and communities, ESDC is undertaking a number of initiatives to improve LMI for and about Indigenous People on and off-reserve:

- Piloting an on-reserve LMI survey, and creating skills inventories for Indigenous communities to help link working-age community members with available jobs;
- Improving sharing of LMI with Indigenous partners by sharing jobs data from the Temporary Foreign Worker Program and the Job Bank, to ensure Indigenous communities have access to information to support their training planning and job placements, and
- Working towards Indigenous LMI sharing processes with Provinces/Territories to maximise the use of internal Indigenous data collected through administrative databases.

To implement these local collaborations and improvements to Indigenous LMI collection, a federal Indigenous statistical institution could be established. This has precedence in Canada—historically, the First Nations Statistical Institute (FNSI) served this purpose on a federal level. In 2015, FNSI was defunded by the Canadian government and ceases to operate now. By reinstituting a statistical institute responsible for data related to Indigenous outcomes, data collection, monitoring and evaluation could be greatly improved. Furthermore, this institution could also benefit Indigenous governments though increased statistical capacity support, reducing administrative costs and increasing interests in local investments (First Nations Statistics Institute, 2004).

In addition, extra resources and supports could be provided to local indigenous organisations to collect data to be used for local planning purposes. Federal surveys could also be designed to generate more local data and estimates for federal policy making and comparative purposes. Currently, the Census provides the largest sample size but it is run only every five years, which limits access to timely, sufficiently disaggregated and sampled information.

Look for opportunities to enhance skills training for Indigenous People through targeted work experience programmes

Gaps in education and skills between Indigenous and non-Indigenous populations leave Indigenous People underrepresented in higher education and much less likely to have acquired a degree or diploma. However, skills training for Indigenous People can improve unemployment rates, job acquisition in knowledge sectors and occupations, and job retention. Currently, federal labour market programmes provides skills training to unemployed Indigenous People and also offers networking opportunities with relevant employers.

Along with skills training programmes, apprenticeships can help in reducing employment rates gaps for Indigenous People. Indigenous People already have a strong and successful presence in the trades. Apprenticeships offer a chance for unemployed Indigenous People to gain educational certification and professional experience in the workplace. These programmes are beneficial in creating further connections between employers and prospective Indigenous employees. There is an opportunity to examine how to continue to expand the use of apprenticeship programmes to assist Indigenous People with job readiness and employers with higher skilled employees.

While federal programming provides helpful training support for unemployed Indigenous People, there could be a greater focus on providing employed Indigenous People with training and skills development to transition to higher-quality, better-paying jobs. Indigenous programming should continue developing flexibilities to support life-long learning opportunities. Through partnerships with employers, federal policies and programmes can provide support in the work environment for Indigenous workers to move up the career ladder. This would assist employers with staff retention and Indigenous employees to gain promotions to new positions through the acquisition of new skills. This means not only supplying technical training certification, but also leadership training to allow Indigenous People to be more represented in managerial positions. This connection to employers could further encourage the hiring of Indigenous People (Employment and Social Development Canada, 2017).

Expand access to higher education opportunities to support Indigenous students

While apprenticeships and VET programmes are generally effective in connecting unemployed Indigenous People to educational certificates and employment, they still do not address equity gaps within the skills system. This is particularly striking within disparities in higher education outcomes. Therefore, there are many benefits to be gained by increasing Indigenous participation and completion of higher education while continuing to address barriers to access and completion of high school.

As shown in this report, the percentage of Indigenous People who have attained a tertiary degree (bachelor's and higher) in Canada is more than 15% lower than the non-Indigenous population (Statistics Canada, 2016). Furthermore, this study demonstrates that outcome gaps in education disadvantage Indigenous People when they enter the workforce; across Canada, the Indigenous population has an 8.4% lower employment rate than non-Indigenous Canadians (Statistics Canada, 2016). However, when considering the employment rate by levels of education, the employment rate gap between the two groups substantially diminishes with each increase in educational level until it is nearly eradicated at the level of tertiary degree attainment (Statistics Canada, 2015).

Currently, federal active labour market programming for Indigenous People addresses these gaps by funding up to two years of post-secondary education for Indigenous students. However, two years is not a sufficient amount of funding to allow Indigenous students to complete four year tertiary degrees if they have no other financial assistance. Federal employment and skills training for Indigenous People should therefore increase the maximum amount of tertiary funding to a ceiling of at least four years for Indigenous students.

Indigenous People are underrepresented in knowledge sectors and occupations. Increases in tertiary attainment allows for greater social and financial mobility for Indigenous People by widening their options of employment to include jobs requiring higher skills. This proposed change within the new ISET programme will help to boost the socio-economic status of participating Indigenous students.

Consider increasing the use of mentorship as a key tool for supporting Indigenous employment

Findings from case studies research have demonstrated that more support could be provided to Indigenous People in the workplace. The Canadian Council for Aboriginal Business 2016 survey indicates that employers have issues finding qualified employees and employee retention. Structural, financial, cultural and institutional barriers associated with Indigenous employment, education and skills show that interventions are needed to address these barriers. Along with life-long learning skills support, Indigenous employees can greatly benefit from mentorship within the workplace.

In terms of implementation, Indigenous mentorship is present to some degree in the Canadian workforce. Employee Resource Groups (ERG) might provide an interesting model in which more mentorship opportunities could be delivered. Traditionally, Employee Resource Groups provide a host of services including mentorship, community events, and personal and professional development consultations. ERGs could offer Indigenous employees a support system and reliable community in a professional setting. By providing reliable, trustworthy mentors and a circle of accountability, the holistic needs of Indigenous People can be addressed in a professional setting.

Outside of the ERG model, it is worth exploring how existing federal actively labour market and skills programmes can encourage more mentorship opportunities in the workplace. Recently, the federal government announced the creation of an Indigenous Mentorship Network Program to facilitate capacity exchange among Indigenous health researchers. This is an interesting model, which could be explored within other sectors of the Canadian economy.

Use social enterprises as a pathway to economic prosperity for Indigenous People

There is an opportunity to further leverage the use of social enterprises to offer new economic opportunities to Indigenous People in Canada. These entities can operate as private entities or non-governmental organisations (NGOs), for instance, to facilitate economic activity that contributes to socioeconomic needs at a local level. Social enterprises can be used an economic development mechanism to gainful employment for Indigenous People in knowledge occupations. Social enterprises managed by Indigenous entrepreneurs will be motivated by more than profits as they will also seek to contribute to their local community. Balancing both social and profitability goals is critical in building stronger and empowered indigenous communities.

Provisions within the *Indian Act* can deter Indigenous entrepreneurs from forming corporations or partnerships on reserves since they are still subjected to taxation. Partially as consequence, 60% of Indigenous enterprises are sole proprietorships. However, for Indigenous entrepreneurs that are not profit-driven, NGOs and social enterprises could provide an appropriate alternative in terms of legal structure. The increase of Indigenous-led NGOs could reduce the burden of financial liability for Indigenous sole proprietors while also answering socioeconomic issues at the local level through untaxed operations. NGOs can also offer further revenue diversification for Indigenous entrepreneurs who have difficulties obtaining bank loans or limited personal funds.

The Neeginan Centre of Winnipeg provides an interesting example of how Indigenous-led social enterprises can transform local communities by addressing barriers to success. Through the Neeginan Centre, a collaboration of Indigenous-led NGOs came together in one physical space to offer services, including but not limited to, Indigenous wellbeing, employment, childcare and education. These organisations recognised needs in their local communities and sought to answer them while providing further employment through their own operations.

References

Canadian Institute of Diversity and Inclusion (2013), "Aboriginal Peoples: Examining Current Practices in the Area of Aboriginal Employee Networks", *Diversity Perspectives*, http://ccdi.ca/wp-content/uploads/2016/06/20130717-CCDI-Report-Aboriginal-ERGs.pdf (accessed on 23 January 2018).

First Nations Statistics Institute (2004), *FNS-SPN: A First Nations Initiative*, 2004, http://www.firststats.ca/faq.asp (accessed on 22 January 2018).

Employment and Social Development Canada (2017), *Engagement on the future of Indigenous labour market programming*, https://www.canada.ca/en/employment-social-development/programs/aboriginal-skills-employment-training-strategy/consultation-skills-employment-training/report-indigenous-labour-market-programming.html (accessed on 22 January 2018).

Statistics Canada (2011), *Public Use Microdata Files (PUMFs), National Household Survey (NHS), 2011*, Author's calculations, http://www12.statcan.gc.ca/nhs-enm/2011/dp-pd/pumf-fmgd/index-eng.cfm (accessed on 30 October 2017).

Statistics Canada (2015), *Aboriginal Peoples: Fact Sheet for Canada*, http://www.statcan.gc.ca/pub/89-656-x/89-656-x2015001-eng.htm (accessed on 23 January 2018).

Statistics Canada (2016), 2016 Census of Population. Canada and census metropolitan areas and census agglomerations, 2016 Census – 25% Sample data, data extracted by Employment and Skills Development Canada, received 11 April 2018.

Statistics Canada (2018), *2016 Census Topic: Aboriginal peoples*, http://www12.statcan.gc.ca/census-recensement/2016/rt-td/ap-pa-eng.cfm (accessed on 22 January 2018).

ORGANISATION FOR ECONOMIC CO-OPERATION AND DEVELOPMENT

The OECD is a unique forum where governments work together to address the economic, social and environmental challenges of globalisation. The OECD is also at the forefront of efforts to understand and to help governments respond to new developments and concerns, such as corporate governance, the information economy and the challenges of an ageing population. The Organisation provides a setting where governments can compare policy experiences, seek answers to common problems, identify good practice and work to co-ordinate domestic and international policies.

The OECD member countries are: Australia, Austria, Belgium, Canada, Chile, the Czech Republic, Denmark, Estonia, Finland, France, Germany, Greece, Hungary, Iceland, Ireland, Israel, Italy, Japan, Korea, Latvia, Luxembourg, Mexico, the Netherlands, New Zealand, Norway, Poland, Portugal, the Slovak Republic, Slovenia, Spain, Sweden, Switzerland, Turkey, the United Kingdom and the United States. The European Union takes part in the work of the OECD.

OECD Publishing disseminates widely the results of the Organisation's statistics gathering and research on economic, social and environmental issues, as well as the conventions, guidelines and standards agreed by its members.

OECD PUBLISHING, 2, rue André-Pascal, 75775 PARIS CEDEX 16
(84 2018 02 1 P) ISBN 978-92-64-30046-0 – 2018

www.ingramcontent.com/pod-product-compliance
Lightning Source LLC
LaVergne TN
LVHW081414110826
845149LV00010B/1741

* 9 7 8 9 2 6 4 3 0 0 4 6 0 *